Gracián meets Góngora
The Theory and Practice of Wit

by

M. J. Woods

Aris & Phillips Ltd – Warminster – England

ISBN 0 85668 657 3

British Library Cataloguing-in-Publication Data
A catalogue record for this book is available from the British Library.

Printed and published in England by Aris & Phillips Ltd, Teddington House, Warminster, Wilts. BA12 8PQ

For Shirley, whose great tolerance I don't deserve, and in memory of Graham, who was such an enthusiast of subtlety.

Contents

Bibliography of Works Cited

Joseph Addison, *The Spectator* (London, 1822), 6 vols

Dámaso Alonso, *Estudios y ensayos gongorinos* (Madrid, Gredos, 1960)

S.L. Bethell, 'Gracián, Tesauro and the nature of Metaphysical wit', in *A Northern Miscellany of Literary Criticism* (Manchester, 1953), pp. 19-40

Max Black, *Models and Metaphors* (Ithaca, New York, 1962)

Mercedes Blanco, *Les rhétoriques de la pointe. Baltasar Gracián et le conceptisme en Europe* (Paris, Champion, 1992)

Dominique Bouhours, *La manière de bien penser dans les ouvrages d'esprit* (Paris 1987)

A. Callejo and M.T. Pajares (eds), Luis de Góngora, *Fabula de Polyfemo y Galathea y Las Soledades. Textos y concordancia* (Madison, Hispanic Seminary of Medieval Studies, 1985)

Antonio Carreira (ed.), Luis de Góngora, *Antología poética* (Madrid, Castalia, 1989)

Benedetto Croce, *Aesthetic,* translated by D. Ainslie (London, Peter Owen, 1967)

Jonathan Culler, *On Deconstruction* (London, Routledge & Kegan Paul, 1983)

Paul de Man, *Allegories of Reading* (New Haven-London, Yale University Press, 1979)

Jacques Derrida, *Margins of Philosophy,* translated by Alan Bass (New York, London, etc, 1982)

Helen Gardner (ed.), *The Metaphysical Poets* (Oxford, Clarendon Press, 1961)

E.J. Gates (ed.), *Documentos gongorinos* (Mexico, Colegio de México, 1960)

Luis de Góngora, *Las firmezas de Isabela,* ed. Robert Jammes (Madrid, Castalia, 1965)

———————— *Polyphemus and Galatea. A study in the interpretation of a baroque poem,* ed. A.A. Parker, with a verse translatiion by Gilbert F. Cunningham, (Edinburgh, Edinburgh University Press, 1977)

———————— , *Obras completas,* ed. Juan and Isabel Millé (Madrid, Aguilar, 1932)

———————— , *Romances,* ed. Antonio Carreño (Madrid. Cátedra, 1985)

Baltasar Gracián, *Obras completas,* ed. Arturo del Hoyo (Madrid, Aguilar, 1960)

———————— , *Agudeza y arte de ingenio,* ed. E. Correa Calderón (Madrid, Castalia, 1969), 2 vols

Hugh H. Grady, 'Rhetoric wit and art in Gracián's Agudeza', *Modern Language Quarterly,* 41 (1980), pp. 21-37

Emilio Hidalgo Serna, *El pensamiento ingenioso en Baltasar Gracián,* Translated from German by Manuel Canet (Barcelona, Anthropos, 1993)

Douglas D. Hofstadter, *Gödel, Escher, Bach: an Eternal Golden Thread* (London, Penguin, 1979)

R. Jakobson, 'Two aspects of language and two types of aphasic disfunction', in *Language in Literature* (Harvard, 1987), Chapter Eight.

Robert Jammes, *Etudes sur l'oeuvre poétique de Don Luis de Góngora y Argote* (Bordeaux, Féret, 1967)

Samuel Johnson, *Lives of the English Poets*, ed. G.B. Hill (Oxford, Clarendon Press, 1905), 3 vols

R.O. Jones, *A Literary History of Spain. The Golden Age: Prose and Poetry* (London, Benn, 1974)

Lebrecht Gotthelf Langbein, *Commentatu de Matthiae Casimiri Sarbievii S.I. Poloni vita studiis et scriptis* (Dresdae, Apud Redericum Hekdium, 1754)

H. Lausberg, *Manual de retórica literaria*, translated by J. Pérez Riesco (Madrid, 1966), Vol II, pp. 144-5

Francisco Leytao Ferreira, *Nova arte de conceitos* (Lisbon, Antonio Pedrozo Cebran, 1718, 1721)

A. Martínez Arancón, *La batalla en torno a Góngora* (Barcelona, Bosch, 1978)

Jacob Masen, *Ars nova argutiarum* (Coloniae Agrippinae, J.A. Kinckium, 1668)

T.E. May, 'Gracián's idea of the concepto', *Hispanic Review*, 18 (1950), 15-41.

——————, *Wit of the Golden Age*,(Kassel, Reichenberger, 1986)

——————, 'An interpretation of Gracián's 'Agudeza y arte de ingenio', *Hispanic Review*, XVI (1948), 275-300

D.G. Morhof, *De arguta dictione* (Lubeck 1705)

L.A. Muratori, *Della perfetta poesia Italiana*, ed. A.M. Salvini (Milan, 1821), 3 vols

Maurice Merleau-Ponty, *Language and Society. Selected Essays of Maurice Merleau-Ponty*. Ed. J. O'Neill (London,1974)

Sforza Pallavicino, *Trattato dello stile e del dialogo* (Rome 1662)

A.A. Parker, '"Concept" and "Conceit": An Aspect of Comparative Literary History', *Modern Language Review*, 77 (1982), xxi-xxxv

Georges Perec, *La disparition* (Paris, Les Lettres Nouvelles, Editions Denoël, 1969)

Matteo Peregrini, *Delle acutezze* (Genoa, 1639)

——————, *Fonti dell'ingegno* (Bologna, 1650)

Denys Petau, *Dionysii Petavii Aurelianensis e societ. Iesu epistolarum* (Paris, 1652)

R.D.F. Pring-Mill, '"Porque yo cerca muriese". An occasional meditation on a conceptista theme', *Bulletin of Hispanic Studies*, 61 (1984), pp. 369-78

Francisco de Quevedo, *Obras completas*, Vol 1, *Poesía original*, ed. J.M. Blecua (Barcelona, Planeta, 1968)

Michael Radau, *Orationes in laudem Befactorum Colegii Vilnensis* (Vilnius, 1640)

——————, *Orator Extemporaneus* (London, 1657)

Ezio Raimondi (ed.), *Trattatisti e narratori del Seicento* (Milan-Naples, Ricciardi, 1960), *La letteratura italiana. Storia e testi*, Vol. 36

I.A. Richards, *The Philosophy of Rhetoric* (Oxford, Oxford University Press, 1978)

Paul Ricoeur, *The Rule of Metaphor,* translated by R. Czerny (London, Routledge & Kegan Paul, 1978)

M. Casimir Sarbiewski,*De acuto et arguto,* in *Wyk łady poetyki. Praecepta poetica,* ed. Stanislaw Skimina (Warsaw-Krakow, 1958), pp. 1-20

Edward Sarmiento, 'Gracián's Agudeza y arte de ingenio', *Modern Language Review,* 27 (1932), pp.280-292 and 420-429

Ferdinand de Saussure, *Cours de linguistique générale,* ed. Tullio de Mauro (Paris, Payot, 1984)

C. Colin Smith, 'An approach to Góngora's Polifemo', *Bulletin of Hispanic Studies,* 42 (1965), pp. 230-38

James Smith, 'On Metaphysical poetry', *Scrutiny,* 3 (1933), pp. 222-39

Carlos Sommervogel (ed.), Agustin and Aloys Backer, *Bibliotèque de la Compagnie de Jésus* (Brussels-Paris, 1890-1932), 11 vols

John Sturrock (ed.), *Structuralism and Since* (Oxford, Oxford University Press, 1979)

Arthur Terry, 'Quevedo and the metaphysical conceit', *Bulletin of Hispanic Studies,* 35 (1958), pp. 211-222

Emmanuele Tesauro, *Il Cannocchiale Aristotelico* (Turin, 1670)

T. Wall, *Casimiri Sarbiewski e societate Jesu Poloniae Poemata Omnia* (Staraviesiae, 1892)

Rosemond Tuve, *Elizabethan and Metaphysical Imagery* (Chicago, University of Chicago Press, 1947)

Ruth Wallerstein, *Studies in Seventeenth-Century Poetic* (Madison-Milwaukee, University of Wisconsin Press, 1965)

George Williamson, *The Proper Wit of Poetry* (London, Faber, 1961)

M.J. Woods, 'Gracian, Peregrini and the theory of Topics', *Modern Language Review,* 58 (1968), pp. 854-863.

———— , *The Poet and the Natural World in the Age of Góngora* (Oxford, Oxford University Press, 1978), pp. 139-44

L.J. Woodward, '*La vida retirada* of Fray Luis de León', *Bulletin of Hispanic Studies,* 31 (1954), pp. 17-26

Introduction

In an age when wit was flourishing on a European scale, none were more famed for their literary wit than the Spanish. Jean Chapelain, President of the French Academy in mid 17th-Century, casting a critical eye across the Pyrenees has some highly disparaging things to say in his letters about the Spaniards' capacity for scholarship, granting them preeminence solely in the field of theology. He suggests that all they were really interested in was wit.[1]

In France wit could be classified as a more or less fringe phenomenon cultivated by a maverick like Cyrano de Bergerac or a light-weight salon poet like Voiture, but alien to the temperament of a Racine. Even in the case of their less conventional poets like Tristan l'Hermite it is whimsy rather than wit which predominates. But in Spain the study of wit takes us into the mainstream of literary activity, encompassing the drama of Calderón, the moralistic prose works of Gracián, the prose satires of Quevedo, and the poetry of both Quevedo and the rival with whom he kept up a bitter enmity, Góngora, the greatest and most controversial poetic genius of the century. In this respect, the situation was not dissimilar to that in England, where wit is not only the most obvious distinguishing feature of the Metaphysical Poets, but is also, in a way which has perhaps been insufficiently recognised, a vital ingredient in Shakespeare's works. Perhaps this recognition might have been more forthcoming if the English had produced a theory of wit of comparable stature to Gracián's.

Within Spain, no poet had a greater reputation for wit than Luis de Góngora. Whether or not this was thought of as enhancing his status depended on how far wit was seen as compatible with decorum. But there is no doubting that Góngora's sharpness is evident across the whole range of his output, whatever the poetic form, and whatever the themes and attitudes expressed. Baltasar Gracián, Spain's theorist of wit, was well aware of this range. In his treatise he drew more illustrations from Góngora than from any other poet, and quoted from a wide variety of texts, including Góngora's play *Las firmezas de Isabela*. Although Góngora's most famous poem, the *Soledades*, is under represented in Gracián's examples, it hardly needs saying today that the poem is a major treasure house of conceits, a fact that was obscured earlier in

---

[1]   "Quant au sçavoir des Espagnols, il y a plus de quarente ans que j'en ay connu le foible dans toute les disciplines ou il n'entre point de théologie, qui n'est pas ma profession...Point de connoissance d'histoire, point de chronologie, point de geographie, point d'art poétique, point d'art d'oratoire. Tout leur fait n'est qu'*agudezas* et en cela ils font consister tout le mérite de l'escrivain', *Lettres de Jean Chapelain de l'Académie Francaise,* ed. P. Tamizey de Larroque, Paris 1880, 2 Vols, II, 255.

this century by the critical tradition of contrasting Quevedo as a cultivator of the conceit, a *conceptista*, and the Góngora of the *Soledades* as a *culteranista*, one who practised a complex style with an idiosyncratic, latinate vocabulary and latinate structures and abundant metaphor.

The superficiality of regarding Góngora's distinguishing features as primarily a matter of style rather than of substance is apparent if one considers one of Góngora *culto* poetic mannerisms, for which he was mocked by Quevedo — the use of the phrase 'si no'. The function of the phrase is to link alternative expressions, sometimes to rule one out in favour of the other, sometimes to give equal weight to both. The frequency of its appearance is symptomatic as much of a habit of thought as it is of a verbal fixation. Making connections between alternative versions of the same phenomena is part of the process of wit, and Góngora's familiar phrase is one means of achieving this.

It is no less superficial to regard metaphor and other instances of figurative language as simply a matter of the mode of expression. Again, the habit of producing metaphors is a habit of making connections between things, linking what is referred to literally on the one hand and figuratively on the other.

The aim of this book is to explore Góngora's genius for ingeniousness in the context of a general theory of both wit and trope. The first two chapters are devoted to the theories of wit of Gracián and his rivals. Unlike the Italian theorists, Gracián, I believe wholly justifiably, did not give trope an essential role in wit. But in practice, Góngora's conceits often embroil us in complex trope. Hence my attempt in Chapters Four and Five to analyse what is going on technically when he uses trope in this involved way. As I argue in Chapter Five, Góngora is often at the interface between literal and figurative language, and the insecurity to which this gives rise can be a powerful source of wit. Superficially this may make it look as if I am aligning myself with critics in the deconstructionist tradition who seek to demonstrate how texts undermine attempts to distinguish between the literal and the figurative. But I do not share their radical linguistic scepticism, which challenges the very idea that there is such a thing as literal language using arguments derived from Saussure's model of how language works. I therefore devote space in Chapter Three to showing the inadequacy of that model and to setting out in more pragmatic terms the relationship between literal language and trope as I see it.

Chapters Six and Seven explore issues raised but not satisfactorily resolved by the theorists of wit. They discuss the role of logic in the conceit, and the question of how one assesses the quality of a conceit, and where the issue of decorum fits into the picture.

Finally, in Chapter Eight I offer a general assessment of the role of wit in Góngora's poetic output as a whole.

Chapter One: Understanding Gracián

The treatise on wit of the Aragonese Jesuit, Baltasar Gracián appeared in two different versions. The first, dated 1642, fifteen years after the death of Luis de Góngora, had as its full title *Arte de ingenio. Tratado de la agudeza en que se explican todos los modos y diferencias de conceptos*.[2] This already introduces us to some key Spanish terms: *ingenio*, translatable as 'wit', and referring to wit as either a faculty of the mind or as a quality found in the products of that faculty; *agudeza*, which, used as a count noun (as in *agudezas* or *una agudeza*), refers to the products of the faculty of wit and is translatable as 'conceit', but which used as a generic noun, as in the title of Gracián's treatise, means the same as *ingenio* — 'wit'; and *conceptos*, which obviously in the context of this title means 'conceits', embodiments of wit, rather than 'concepts'. A usable translation for *agudeza* used as a generic term is 'sharp-mindedness', so that we could translate Gracián's title here as *The art of wit. A treatise on sharp-mindedness in which are explained all the different types of conceit*. Or again, in the case of Gracián's revised treatise, appearing in 1648 with the main title *Agudeza y arte de ingenio*, one could render the title as *Sharp-mindedness and the Art of Wit*.

What this second treatise offers is a expanded version with many more illustrations. It also makes a number of finer distinctions as the number of detailed sub-types of conceit is enlarged. These extra complications make the new version in some ways more obscure. But neither version is easy to approach, as Gracián himself recognised when he concluded his introductory remarks to the reader by expressing the hope that his book will have the good fortune to meet somebody capable of understanding it. This chapter will attempt to deal with some of the difficult issues posed by Gracián's sometimes irritating treatise in the belief that perseverance is well worth while and that Gracián has significant advantages over some other theorists.

At the root of Gracián's theory lies his account of what exactly it is that we appreciate when we enjoy wit of any kind. It is, he tells us, a kind of beauty ('algún sutilísimo artificio').[3] The word he uses, *artificio*, suggests an artistically created beauty, and indeed he sees it as analogous to the symmetry to be appreciated in architecture, or the harmony in music. But whereas in these two cases it is a physical relationship that is being admired, in the case of wit, the pattern involved is

---

2   The text is reproduced in Arturo del Hoyo's edition of the *Obras completas* (Madrid, Aguilar, 1960), pp. 1162-1254.

3   *Agudeza y arte de ingenio,* ed. E. Correa Calderón (Madrid, Castalia, 1969), 2 vols, Vol I, p. 53.

at a more abstract, purely intellectual level, and hence superior ('el [artificio] superlativo de todos'), and is later referred to by Gracián as an intellectual symmetry.

Gracián uses a number of related terms to refer to and describe this special beauty, the chief of which is *correspondencia*, correspondence. Others are *concordancia, correlación, conformidad, conveniencia, proporción*. What they all have in common is that they involve the idea of a pleasing mutual relationship between different elements. Wit involves a kind of fit or match.

It is worth pausing at this stage to note that Gracián does not imply that the relationship in question has to be one of similarity. He makes it clear at an early stage that correspondence is an appropriate term to use even where elements are contrasted because this still connects things together in a pleasing way.[4] His point is a cogent one, since complementaries, yin and yang, can be said to match each other in a satisfying way. But more than that, we need to free ourselves from the prison of the English critical tradition which starts in the 18th Century with the analysis of wit in the Metaphysical poets in terms of a search for likeness in things which are unlike. As soon as we start to think of correspondence in terms of a comparison between different things which is concerned basically with similarities and dissimilarities we make difficulties for ourselves and place unnecessary barriers between ourselves and Gracián. I shall illustrate this point later when studying the details of Gracián's method. In the meantime it is worth making the cautionary observation that one of the great merits of his basic theory is its generality, a feature we lose if we interpret *correspondencia* too narrowly.

Conversely, *correspondencia* in Gracián's sense is not to be understood so widely as to include any kind of beautiful correspondence whatsoever. The correspondences noted by him in architecture and music are seen as analogous but inferior to those of wit. In terms of the psychology of Gracián's day with its strong Thomistic flavour, the superiority of wit derives from its use of the superior faculty of the mind, the intellect, as opposed to the lower part involved in the processing of sensory information. The correspondences in architecture and music are between physical, sensually apprehended elements.

There is, however, a difficulty with Gracián's argument here. One could object that these relations between physical elements are ultimately mathematical and hence abstract in nature and hence processable only by the intellect. It is equally true that the correspondences of wit can only be conveyed through a physical medium and perforce use the 'lower', sensory part of the mind.

Nevertheless, there is, I suspect, a valid distinction to be made between the intellectual appreciation of physical symmetry, and the appreciation of intellectual beauty in physical phenomena. It is surely not Gracián's intention to rule out the possibility of wit in music and the visual arts, particularly bearing in mind that in

---

[4]   'Esta correspondencia es genérica a todos los conceptos, y abraza todo el artificio del ingenio, que aunque éste sea tal vez por contraposición y disonancia, aquello mismo es artificiosa conexión de los objetos', *ed..cit.*, (I, 56).

his treatise he does not restrict his examples to wit manifested through language, but also includes witty action as one of his genres. To take the case of music, one might distinguish between the beautiful correspondences of harmony, and those of counterpoint which are more consciously intellectual. There is surely wit in the dazzling ingenuity of counterpoint in J.S. Bach's Musical Offering.[5] Again the musical form of theme and variations lends itself to wit in its treatment. This same artistic form is exploitable in a whole variety of arts, including, for example, the culinary art. Gracián mentions the ability of the human palate to appreciate different combinations of tastes as an instance of correspondence that falls short of wit. But a meal could equally well show wit in relationships recognized by the intellect rather than the palate, by, for example, allusions or disguises in the way the food is presented.

One other aspect of *correspondencia* apart from its beauty and its intellectual nature is its subtlety. In fact, Gracián from time to time uses *sutileza* as an alternative term to *agudeza* to mean a manifestation of wit. This implies that the correspondences of wit are not obvious. Rather than describe them as surprising, which can have the disadvantage of relying too heavily on audience response, Gracián very sensibly identifies an objective quality in the relationships of wit themselves.

Thus far I have talked slightly vaguely of the *correspondencia* of wit being a relationship between elements. We now need to consider what these elements are. At one stage, having cited an epigram of Martial's joking that a doctor having turned gravedigger is still pursuing the same line of work, Gracián writes:

> Bien patente está la correspondencia entre médico y sepulturero, perseverando en su ejercico de echar en la sepultura. Hállase symmetría intelectual entre los términos del pensamiento, tanto más primorosa que la material entre columnas y acróteras, cuánto va del objecto del ingenio, al de un sentido. (I, 67)

Instead of the physical correspondence between architectural features in the epigram we have an abstract, and hence in Gracián's view superior, correspondence between what are referred to as the terms of thought or of the thought. And these terms are the objects apprehended by wit as an intellectual faculty. In the case of literary wit the thought might be a proposition, or even a set of propositions forming an argument insofar as Gracián apparently regards a whole poem as capable of constituting a single thought.[6] But we should beware of assuming that the terms of such a thought can necessarily be identified with what a logician would regard as the terms of the proposition or propositions, their subjects or predicates. In the case of the epigram just cited, for example, 'doctor' and 'gravedigger' are better regarded as

---

5   See the introduction of Douglas D. Hofstadter's *Gödel, Escher, Bach: an Eternal Golden Thread* (London, Penguin, 1979)

6   'Aunque encierre en si dos o tres agudezas, con todo eso se llama incompleja, porque va por modo de un pensamiento solo.' (I, 62).

subjects of discourse for investigation. For Gracián, the terms of thought are the attributes which are found to match during the investigative process. In this case it is the effects of both professions which are matched.

Gracián's approach is explained in Discurso IV, where he describes the production of wit from the perspective of the writer searching for a correspondence between the attributes pertaining to the subject of discourse, where the subject is represented as a kind of centre radiating pointers to the features which will provide the potential basis for a correspondence:

> Es el sujeto sobre quien se discurre y pondera ... uno como centro, de quien reparte el discurso líneas de ponderación a las entidades que lo rodean; estos es, a los adjuntos que lo coronan, como son sus causas, sus efectos, atributos, calidades, contingencias, circunstancias de tiempo, lugar, modo, etc., y cualquiera otro término correspondiente (I, 64)

These features are then compared until a match is found which is then given expression in a subtle way which sets it into relief ('pondérala')

> valos careando de uno en uno con el sujeto, y unos con otros, entre sí; y en descubriendo alguna conformidad o conveniencia que digan, ya con el principal sujeto, ya unos con otros, exprímela, pondérala, y en esto está la sutileza. (I, 64)

Gracián uses a variety of technical terms to refer generally to these attributes. One of these is 'extremos', which clearly does not mean 'extremes', but is equivalent to 'términos' (terms), as the following phrase makes clear when it refers to the connection between the mutually related 'extremos' or 'términos' of the subject: 'la connexion de los extremos o términos correlatos del sujeto, repito causas, efectos, adjuntos, circunstancias, contingencias' (I, 89). No doubt Gracián's choice of the word 'extremo' was influenced by the way he represents the subject of discourse as a centrally placed entity surrounded by peripheral entities which can be seen as 'extremos' in that they are diagramatically speaking not central but on the outer edge.

Sometimes Gracián uses a qualifying adjective with the noun 'extremos' in generally referring to the attributes being related, as, for example, when he talks of 'los extremos objectivos del concepto, que son los correlatos' (I, 59). Here the expression 'extremos objectivos' seems to be equivalent to the term 'objectos' which Gracián also uses from time to time, the objects in question being not material objects, which are handled by the lower faculties, but abstract objects manipulable by the intellect.

Gracián also refers to 'los extremos cognoscibles', (cognizable terms), an indication that abstract though they may be, the terms grasped by the intellect offer some sort of handle on reality. In terms of the standard psychological theory of Gracián's time, this is because the intellect ultimately derives the material it works on from the experience of the senses as stored in the memory. In his final chapter Gracián looks at wit in terms of its 'causes' in the Aristotelian sense, and in dealing with the 'material cause' implies that the relationships investigated by wit exist independently of their discovery by the investigating mind.[7]

Having discovered a match between elements in the subject of discourse the artist clearly then has to communicate it to others. The interpretation of Gracián's account of this stage of the creative process has given rise to major problems and disagreements between the critics as to how some of the key Spanish terms are to be understood and how they should be rendered in English.

One thing on which there can be no dispute is that the end product which embodies the correspondence can always be described in Gracián's terminology as an *agudeza*. Most critics seem content to render this in English as 'conceit', although A.A. Parker holds that not all *agudezas* are conceits, apparently on the grounds that traditionally the term 'conceit' is applied more restrictively to cases of complex metaphor.[8] My own view is that such a critical tradition, if there is one, is not worth preserving in view of the lack of any suitable alternative term to 'conceit' in English for referring to an *agudeza* which is not based on complex metaphor. It is simply too ponderous to constantly have to use a phrase such as 'manifestation of wit' to translate *agudeza* when one can simply use the term 'conceit' with appropriate qualifying adjectives in cases where there is any likelihood of misunderstanding. My own practice, therefore, will be to use the term 'conceit' to mean quite generally any manifestation of wit.

Gracián's use of the term *concepto*, which at first glance looks as if it ought to be equivalent to the English word 'conceit', has given rise to much confusion. In the early chapters, including Discurso II where he offers his famous definition of the *concepto* which we shall examine shortly, Gracián seems to make a distinction between the *agudeza* as end-product and the *concepto* either as something preparatory to the final *agudeza* or as something embodied in but distinct from the *agudeza*. Hence he may talk of a particular type of *agudeza* embodying a particular kind of *concepto*. However, there is no attempt on Gracián's part to use the term consistently in a special sense, and it is evident that more often than not he uses the *agudeza* and *concepto* interchangeably.

Gracián is aware that *concepto* is a multi-purpose word which can be used outside the context of wit simply to mean 'concept'. For example, when he distinguishes between what he calls the *agudeza de concepto* and the *agudeza verbal*, the expression *de concepto* obviously has to mean 'conceptual' rather than 'witty'. He draws our attention to the fact that in the special sense in which he usually uses the term *concepto* in this treatise it implies the presence of wit:

Las [desemejanzas] conceptuosas, y que son rigurosamente conceptos...(I, 145)

---

7   La materia es fundamento del discurrir; ella da pie a la sutileza. Están ya en los objetos mismos las agudezas objetivas, especialmente los misterios, reparos, crisis, si se obró con ellas; llega y levanta la caza el ingenio.' (II, 255)

8   '"Concept" and "Conceit": An Aspect of Comparative Literary History', *Modern Language Review,* 77 (1982), xxi-xxxv

One context in which Gracián makes no distinction whatsoever between the two terms is in referring to the different categories of wit classified by him. For example, Discurso XXXII refers to *la agudeza por paronomasia* in the chapter heading but to 'esta especie de concepto' in the first paragraph, and 'el artificio destos conceptos' in the following one, but reverts to the term *agudeza* later, talking of 'la variedad destas agudezas' (II, 48), and in the chapter headings generally there is no consistency in the use of the two terms.

Turning now to the definition of the *concepto* in its context in Discurso II, Gracián has been explaining the nature of beauty in wit as a harmonious relationship pertaining between elements which the understanding grasps and gives expression to:

> Consiste, pues, este artificio conceptuoso, en una primorosa concordancia, en una armónica correlación entre dos o tres cognoscibles extremos, expresada por un acto del entendimiento. (I, 55)

After an interpolated example, he adds:

> De suerte que se puede definir el concepto: Es un acto del entendimiento, que exprime la correspondencia que se halla entre los objectos. La misma consonancia o correlación artificiosa exprimida, es la sutileza objectiva, como se ve, o se admira, en este célebre soneto...

Gracián's comment at the end here that the sonnet he is about to quote is or contains 'la sutileza objectiva', a conceit in objective form, can be seen as an acknowledgment that once the correspondence perceived by the artist has been given a form of words then it is publicly available and can serve as an object to be processed by the reader's intellect. Up to that point it is at most a virtual conceit in the mind of the artist. In other words, the verb 'exprimir' seems to refer to an act of externalization rather than some private inner process taking place within the artist. The point is an important one, because 'exprimir' in some contexts could refer to an inner process of mental representation. Thomistic psychology distinguished between 'species impressa' or ideas imprinted by sensory stimuli on a passive mind, and 'species expressa', or ideas formed by the intellect actively manipulating the material available to it.

T.E. May in his analysis of the rationale underlying the distinction between the concepto as an intellectual act and the *agudeza* notes:

> The basis of his theory is an attempt to respect the fact that the conceit is primarily, for him, an experience. When he comes to consider the conceit in detail, the situation is resolved in this way: the conceit is seen now, not as a *concepto*, but as an *agudeza*, a single complex object, corresponding to a past completed experience; and in it Gracián is able to point to a multiplicity of relationships which he can then use to describe it. But the original intuitive *concepto* escapes close definition.[9]

---

[9]   'Gracián's idea of the concepto', *Hispanic Review,* 18 (1950), 15-41. Reprinted in T.E. May, *Wit of the Golden Age,*(Kassel, Reichenberger, 1986) pp. 53-79, from which I quote (p 68).

There may be another motive, however, for Gracián's desire to distinguish between *concepto* and *agudeza*. At first glance the distinction might seem to have little practical value. If a *concepto* is the action taken by the mind as it produces an *agudeza* then there can be no independent existence for either. Where there is a *concepto* then we have the birth of an *agudeza*. Where there is an *agudeza* there must have been a prior *concepto* the only evidence for which from the audience's point of view lies in the final *agudeza*. But if we think of the *concepto* as the general conception of a structure of thought rather than merely a prior rehearsal of words one is about to use then it may have more than a mere curiosity value in a theory of wit. There are occasional clues that Gracián wishes to distinguish between the basic conception underlying a conceit and its execution in practice. For example, Gracián comments on one technique when executed, 'declárase más el concepto' (I, 181) which suggests that the *concepto* is a basic idea capable of being expressed with varying degrees of clarity. Again, the *agudeza* may offer a hint as to an underlying idea rather than expressing it overtly:

> Tal vez no se hace la ponderación de propósito, conténtase con apuntar,
> que si la razón is valiente, bien se deja conocer el concepto. (I, 89)

Indeed, it makes perfect sense to distinguish between the *concepto* as a plan, and the *agudeza* as one of a number of possible implementations of it. For instance, an example of a witty action given by Gracián of the Duke of Savoy drawing his sword in response to a request for his credentials (I, 59) could equally well have taken a verbal form with the Duke saying "My sword, Sir, can provide all the evidence you need". Yet despite their different medium, both examples could be said to embody the same *concepto*.

A radically different interpretation of the term *concepto* has been advanced by Professor A.A. Parker in his article 'Concept and conceit' which drives a wedge not only between *concepto* and *agudeza* but even between the *concepto* and wit. In the following paragraphs I shall address some of the issues raised by his unconventional approach.

Noting that critics who are not specialists in Spanish have been puzzled by Gracián's definition of the *concepto* as 'an act of the understanding which expresses the relationship between objects', Parker asks:

> Is this not really a definition of ordinary metaphor? Hispanists, beginning with Sarmiento, have themselves been puzzled by the fact that Gracián never states that a *concepto* has an essential relation to trope. This difficulty has caused trouble even to May. The difficulties, I suggest, disappear when we realize that a *concepto* does not have to be a conceit, but is basically an idea or thought, and that Gracián's relationships do not have to be metaphorical but can be many types of intellectual contrasts, similarities or identifications.[10]

---

[10]   *Op.cit.*, xxx

Parker suggests here that the main cause of bemusement for the reader is that Gracián has apparently defined an ordinary metaphor instead of the complex metaphor traditionally associated with the conceit. But there must surely be few readers naive enough to succumb to the twisted logic of thinking that because a metaphor expresses a relationship between things then one can define a metaphor as anything which expresses a relationship between things. The essential ingredients which characterise metaphor, both missing from Gracián's definition of the *concepto*, are that the relationship must be one of similarity and that it must be expressed figuratively and not literally. What Parker fails to point out is that to make sense of Gracián, not only do we need to recognize that *correspondencia* is not limited to the relationship of similarity, but we also must recognize the verb *exprimir* includes a number of different possible modes of expression and is not limited to figurative expression. It is not even limited to verbal expression. But at the same time, Gracián's treatise makes little sense if we widen the scope of *correspondencia* in another direction to include virtually any relationship between things. For Gracián *correspondencia* embodied a special intellectual beauty and excluded the ordinary and dull, whether it be an ordinary metaphor or an ordinary anything else. Parker's failure to recognize this I believe constitutes a fundamental flaw in his approach.

I suspect the real surprise for most readers approaching Gracián's definition is that they were expecting a description of the conceit as the end product of the artist's endeavour, and are given instead what looks like a description of the mental act of actually creating that end product. We might be tempted to wonder whether *acto* really has to mean an action or whether it is not being used metonymically to refer to the result of an action, in the same way that an act of Parliament is not an activity but the result of an activity. This would in effect make *concepto* and *agudeza* co-terminous. But if we feel that Gracián is trying to preserve a distinction between the two, and grant the *concepto* a mental status, then what is wrong with Parker's suggestion that it means 'concept' rather than 'conceit'? We need to follow his analysis a little further to see the problem.

> In Gracián's definition the *concepto* is presented only as an act of the understanding; if elevated by *ingenio* to *agudeza*, it then becomes a witty concept which may or may not be a conceit. I realize that this distinction is strained, but the strain results from the present-day sense of 'conceit'. It seems sensible to translate Gracián's *concepto* simply as 'concept', making it clear that this is 'concept' in a special sense. Gracián's evidently means by *concepto* not the notion of a class or a single object, but a statement or proposition of some kind, in particular a thought or assertion that establishes a conceptual relationship. A concept is therefore a thought that provokes further thought, which may or may not be witty.[11]

---

[11]   *Op.cit.*, xxx

Evidently, as Parker points out, Gracián cannot be defining a concept in its standard sense. Indeed, it is not normal to think of a concept expressing anything. It is more usual to see a statement as embodying and expressing concepts. But the main difficulty is that Parker still does not seem to interpret the sense of *concepto* as special enough. It is surely insufficient to see it as 'a thought that establishes a conceptual relationship'. The relationship in question needs to be a *correspondencia*, and as such reveals the special subtle beauty which characterizes wit. The *concepto* in its special sense is a *correspondencia* as apprehended by the mind as it contemplates the possibility of producing an *agudeza* based on it. The three terms are thus inseparable. There can be no *agudeza* without a *concepto*, and no *concepto* without a *correspondencia*. The *agudeza* embodies a *concepto*, and the *concepto* embodies a *correspondencia*.

Taking Gracián's definition of the *concepto* in its context, it is clear that in a work whose avowed subject is wit, and in the middle of a discussion in Discurso II about what constitutes the essence of wit it would have been a meaningless irrelevance for him to then have embarked on out of the blue a definition of the *concepto* as a mental concept falling short of wit. For Gracián, the *concepto* makes its appearance once the search for a beautiful correspondence has been concluded. Parker seems to see the *concepto* as still part of the preliminary investigatory process and as capable of further extension and elaboration. But there is nothing in Gracián's text to support this approach.

There are dangers, then, in taking Gracián's definition out of context. Moreover, it would be a mistake to invest too much importance in this phrase of his which flows naturally from what has gone before and treat it as if it were designed to stand on its own as an encapsulation of his entire theory. It is significant that the famous definition does not appear at all in his first version of the treatise.

Once Gracián has outlined the basic theory applying to all conceits he proceeds in Discurso III to consider how different types of conceit can be classified, arriving at four broad categories each with a number of sub-categories. He also considers how the different types may be combined.

Although we shall not be examining here the detailed workings of the whole scheme, it is worth making clear the general principles underlying it and discussing some of the problems arising from Gracián's exposition of the various types.

The four basic types identified by Gracián are the *agudeza de correlación*, the *agudeza de ponderación*, the *agudeza de raciocinación*, and the *agudeza de invención*. These are not mutually exclusive, and a conceit which combines more than one type is termed an *agudeza mixta* as opposed to an *agudeza pura*. However one consequence of Gracián's general theory which he does not spell out is that since *correlación*, alias *correspondencia*, is common to all conceits then all must belong automatically to the first type, the *agudeza de correlación*. Some may have extra features which make them simultaneously members of one or more of the other types as 'mixed' conceits.

The *agudeza de correlación* is further subdivided into those conceits in which the correspondence is positive (*agudezas de proporción*) and those where it is negative (*agudezas de improporción*). Their generic nature is pointed out at the end of Discurso V. In talking of the negative one, Gracián uses a terminology very reminiscent of the definition of wit found in other theorists and favoured by many modern critics as a *discordia concors*: 'Hacen estos conceptos una disonancia muy concorde entre los correlatos'. In the last sentence of Discurso II Gracián makes the point that even wit which is built on contrast embodies a beautiful correspondence: 'aunque éste (artificio) sea tal vez por contraposición y disonancia, aquello mismo es artificiosa conexión de los objectos.' But he does not insist on an element of tension as a requirement for a good conceit. In the *agudeza de proporción* there is pure harmony without any discordant element.

Gracián's exposition of the *agudeza por semejanza*, one of the sub-types of *agudeza de proporción*, requires some explanation both because Gracián singles it out as special and because this type of conceit has been seen as particularly problematic by T.E. May in his analysis of Gracián's theory. To produce this type of conceit according to Gracián one confronts the subject not with its own adjacent entities but with 'un término extraño, como imagen, que le exprime su ser o le representa sus propriedades, efectos, causas, contingencias y demás adjuntos; no todos, sino algunos, o los más principales.' (I, 114)

May's comments on this are difficult to penetrate, and are based partly on the analysis of one of Gracián's examples in which Martial quips to a critic of his poems "I prefer the dishes at my supper to have pleased the guests rather than the cooks". May notes Gracián's lack of concern with the series dishes-supper-guests, and the way he refrains from looking at this as built up from simple trope, and his identification of the centre of interest as the word 'cooks'. May concludes that

> the conceit *por semejanza* is a conceit of proportion turned, as it were on
> its side; for in the conceit of proportion interest centres upon the
> proportion, the correlation of subject and adjacents; whereas in the
> *semejanza* the interest centres not on any proportion or improportion, but
> upon the comparison.[12]

May seems to imply that the same basic material can be approached from two quite different perspectives. That of the *agudeza de proporción* sees a conceit as built upon an analogy which may take us through a sequence of logical steps typified by the kind of extended comparison underlying Góngora's sonnet 'Arbol de cuyos ramos' (Millé 256). Whereas that of the *agudeza por semejanza* ignores this kind of multiplicity, even if, as in the case of the example from Martial, there is a perceptible logical series, and focuses instead in a more unified vision on what is psychologically the nub of the conceit.

---

12   'An interpretation of Gracián's 'Agudeza y arte de ingenio', *Hispanic Review*, XVI
      (1948), 275-300, reprinted in T.E. May, *Wit of the Golden Age*, *Op.cit.*, pp. 3-28,
      from which I quote (p. 12).

One problem with May's view here is that the *agudeza de proporción* is identified by Gracián as generic. It cannot legitimately be contrasted with the *agudeza por semejanza* which is one of its sub-types. *Proporción* here means simply 'positive correspondence', whether simple or complex. There is no requirement that it relate more than two elements or that there should be some sort of series.

Another objection to May's approach is that Gracián's description of the *agudeza por semejanza* in terms of two subjects instead of one suggests that Gracián approaches it from a more complicated perspective than that envisaged by May. The following pair of examples can serve as an illustration of how Gracián's contrast between a single and double subject works. Firstly, take Góngora's description of a cruel girl as a typical product of her native land as quoted by Gracián:

> Hija al fin de sus arenas
> engendradoras de sierpes (I, 64)[13]

The subject of discourse here is a single one, the girl, and Góngora's conceit makes a connection between her attribute of cruelty and the circumstance of the place where she was born. Although there is an implicit likeness here between her harmfulness and that of the local fauna there is no direct connection in terms of a simile or metaphor between her and the serpents. The conceit is subtler than that, and its vital ingredient is provided by the connection of the circumstance of place.

My second example is from the opening dedication of Góngora's *Soledades* where he says of the animals killed in the hunt 'espumoso coral le dan al Tormes', thereby describing their blood flowing into the river. The subject of discourse in this case is the blood, and the 'extraneous term', the coral. Here the connection is sought between the surrounding attributes, circumstances, etc. of blood on the one hand and coral on the other. The shared attribute of similar colour offers no interest from the point of view of wit, for it lacks the necessary intellectual beauty. In this case the special circumstance of the blood flowing into the water provides the necessary point of interest. As in the other example the correspondence is based on the circumstance of place.

The fact that in this second example the relationship is expressed metaphorically is of no concern since the same correspondence could have been expressed in literal terms as a simile rather than a metaphor. The mode of expression need not affect the structure of the conceit but is largely a question of the medium through which one has chosen to express it.

One way of contrasting the two examples above is to say that whereas the first one has only one effective subject, the second has two — the blood, and the subsidiary one of the coral. In the first instance, a comparison is made between the girl's attributes and her circumstances: in the second, alongside the common colour of blood and coral which is taken for granted, the special circumstance of blood

---

13   See Luis de Góngora, *Obras completas,* ed. Juan and Isabel Millé, (Madrid, Aguilar, 1932), No. 17, p. 71.

flowing into the river is compared with the normal circumstance of coral being aquatic.

Thus far we have concentrated on and examined the issues relating to Gracián's most basic type of conceit, the *agudeza de correlación*. It remains for us to see what are the extra ingredients which characterise the remaining three categories of *agudeza* for Gracián.

Understanding the principles which underlie Gracián's second main type of conceit, the *agudeza de ponderación juiciosa sutil*, to give it its full name, is one of the more difficult challenges posed by his treatise. For some English speaking critics the process has not been helped by their assumption that *la ponderación* and its corresponding verb, *ponderar*, which occurs so frequently in this treatise, refer to some kind of pondering. True, in Spanish *ponderar* can sometimes mean 'ponder', but more often it is synonymous with the verb *encarecer*, in the sense of 'to express in superlative terms'. We can contrast the two meanings in general terms by saying that the first involves a process of mulling something over, and is exploratory, tentative and imperfective in nature, whereas the second is assertive, communicates a conclusion reached, and is perfective in nature. In terms of the underlying metaphor of weight implied in the etymology of *ponderar*, the first sense is of weighing something up, whilst the second is of adding weight to something. It is clear from some of the grammatical constructions used by Gracián, such as 'ponderar que', as well as from general considerations of consistency that this second sense is the one which prevails in the *Agudeza y arte de ingenio*. But even when we have understood this, there are still problems in grasping the rationale underlying the demarcation of main types and sub-types of conceit in relation to the *agudeza de ponderación*.

One confusing thing is that already in Discurso IV, which is supposed to be concerned solely with the pure *agudeza de proporción* of Type 1, Gracián's prose is peppered with instances of the verb *ponderar* and the noun *ponderación*. At one stage it is quite clear that he is jumping the gun, and introducing material which belongs later when he writes:

> Mas si sólo exprimir esta correspondencia y armonía, que se halla entre los extremos objectivos, es sutileza y obra grande del pensar, qué será cuando no se contente con eso sólo un grande ingenio, sino que pase adelante y llegue a realzarla? Prodigio es del sutilizar. Puédese adelantar de muchos modos: sea el primero añadiendo la ponderación a la correlación. (I, 70)

Obviously, what Gracián is describing here is an enhancement which raises conceits above the level of the basic type and makes it an *agudeza de ponderación*. It may well be that when he came to look for illustrations of the basic type of conceit that he could find insufficient suitable examples, and that the majority of ones which occurred to him were of a more complex nature.

The complexity of many conceits in practice means that it was often open to Gracián to categorize particular examples under any one of a number of different headings. This is a situation which he does not handle particularly well, and in general the structure of his exposition is confusing. For example, his discussion of the *agudeza de semejanza*, to judge by Gracián's list of sub-types of the *agudeza pura*, ought logically to have followed hard on the heels of the *agudeza de improporción*. But its appearance is delayed for reasons which can best be surmised by looking at the original version of Gracián's theory, the *Arte de ingenio* of 1642, with its simpler structure. Looking at the chapter headings from Discurso IV onwards in this treatise we have the following sequence: 'De los conceptos de correspondencia y proporción', 'De la agudeza de improporción y disonancia', 'De los conceptos de misterio', 'De la agudeza de reparo', 'De los conceptos sobre semejanza', 'De las semejanzas que se fundan en misterio o reparo'. The conceits in this last chapter could have been classed under either *semejanza* or under *misterio* or *reparo*. By classifying them under *semejanza* Gracián creates a difficulty for himself. Until he has expounded what he means by *conceptos de misterio* and *reparo* we will not understand his exposition of these compound conceits of *semejanza*, hence the need to interpolate two chapters which interrupt the flow and introduce material which otherwise would have been better placed later in the treatise.

Where this particular material should best have gone is problematic. Gracián's initial listing of sub-types places *misterios* and *reparos* in category three, as *conceptos de raciocinación*. Yet the language Gracián uses in discussing them, and, indeed, the new chapter headings in his 1648 version of the treatise, seem to place them firmly within Type 2, the *agudeza de ponderación juiciosa sutil*. The issue is worth pursuing as this will sharpen our understanding of the principles underlying the categorization of conceits.

A large number of conceits discussed by Gracián take the form of an explanation or justification of the correspondence on which they are founded. Often they consist of two parts, the first of which poses a problem or at least suggests that there is some explaining to be done, and the second of which is the actual explanation which resolves the difficulty.

Obviously such a two-part rational process could be regarded as a kind of argument which is akin to a proof. It is thus not unreasonable to include them along with 'proofs' under the heading *agudeza de raciocinación*. But parts one and two of such conceits can take a variety of different forms, and if we focus on these individual forms instead of on the dual structure of the conceit taken as a whole we may find examples of a kind of highlighting or emphasis which could be classed as *ponderación*.

In fact Gracián does use the term *ponderación* as a general term to refer to stage one in such conceits. Of the two parts, this is the less important:

> Dos formalidades, o dos partes, incluye esta agudeza: la una es la ponderación, y la otra la razón que se da, y ésta es la principal. (I, 89)

The *ponderación* may in fact follow the explanation rather than precede it, or may be only implied rather than outwardly expressed.[14] That is to say, an explanation may pre-empt or be the implicit answer to a question not directly expressed. As for the forms which it may take, it may simply challenge us to consider why a particular set of circumstances is the case, as in the *agudeza por ponderación misteriosa*. It may suggest that there is a problem in accepting the relationship which ultimately will be explained, as in the *agudeza por ponderación de dificultad*. It may even suggest that there is some contradiction in the proposed correspondence, and in his original treatise Gracián reserved the term *reparo*, translatable here as 'objection', for an observation pointing out such a contradiction. However in the revised version we find Gracián using the term *reparo* in a less restricted sense to mean a pointed observation which may or may not direct our attention to a contradiction.

As for the second part of these dual conceits, the explanation, Gracián refers to it variously as 'la razón que se da', 'la solución','la salida' or 'el desempeño', which literally means the redeeming of pawned goods, but which in this abstract sense refers to the escape from a difficulty. Thus *desempeños*, which figure on the list of sub-types of the *agudeza de ponderación* imply the posing of a problem from which these explanations offer an escape.[15]

We find Gracián using the term *ponderación* to apply not only to the process of posing the problem but also to various methods of resolving it which may be emphatic in nature. For example, the *sentencia*, a weighty saying, may offer an impressive resolution of a difficulty, and Gracián praises conceits based on simile, 'cuando la semejanza va realzada con el misterio, y se le da salida con una grave y sentenciosa ponderación' (I, 141). Hence it is a type of *ponderación* which makes us aware of the mystery, and another type of *ponderación* which resolves the mystery with a pithy expression.

These are some of the complications, then, in Gracián's handling of complex conceits which are susceptible to multiple classification. It remains for us to consider the nature of the *agudeza de invención*, the fourth and final type of conceit, whose sub-types include 'ficciones, estratagemas, invenciones en acción y dichos'. These latter *invenciones* involve wit produced on the spur of the moment in real-life situations, and include retorts ('las prontas retorciones'), and witty actions, whose inclusion shows the breadth of Gracián's conception of wit. What Gracián understands by 'stratagems' is less clear, however, and these do not seem to be discussed separately. The discussion of 'ficciones' in Discurso XXXV, 'De los conceptos por ficción', starts off by seeing poetic fictions as basically a vehicle for enhancing *la ponderación*, 'aumentando con lo fingido la ponderación' (II, 69). This rather undermines the validity of seeing the fictional conceit as a type of conceit in

---

14   'Tal vez no se hace la ponderación de propósito... También la razón que se le da al misterio puede preceder a la ponderación y reparo', (I, 89)

15   Compare Gracián's comment on *las ponderaciones de contrariedad*: 'como se funda en contrariedad y disonancia, sobresale mucho el empeño' (I, 108).

its own right, although Gracián does eventually state that it is capable of standing alone: 'Aunque no tenga otra agudeza mixta, la ficción sola es bastante para sutileza' (II, 77). Feigning is also a technique that can be used in the production of other types of conceit. Thus Discurso XV, which seems to be an adjunct to the previous one which concerns conceits based on parallels, discusses the 'careo condicional, fingido y ayudado', where the writer achieves the necessary correspondence by having resource to hypothetical or fictional situations. Discursos XX and XXI are related in a similar way, with the first dealing with 'los encarecimientos conceptuosos' and the second with 'los encarecimientos condicionales, fingidos y ayudados'.

In the second part of his two-part treatise, Gracián moves from considering the various sub-types of wit to looking at things on a larger scale. Part Two is concerned with the *agudeza compuesta*, or compound conceit, in which the combination of various individual conceits into an ingenious whole can be considered as a large-scale conceit in itself. Hence an entire work of fiction might be considered as a complex conceit, and obvious case in point being Gracián's own allegorical novel, *El Criticón*, in which a host of individual conceits are worked into an ingenious framework in which the contrasting rational and instinctive aspects of human behaviour are separated and externalized in the two protagonists of the novel, Andrenio and Critilo. On a smaller scale, a sonnet as a whole based on a single ingenious idea may include further individual conceits and constitute a complex conceit. Góngora's sonnet 'La dulce boca' (Millé 238) could be considered a case in point.

Gracián's conception of the *agudeza compleja* contributes to the argument that it is legitimate to consider a general strategy independently of its detailed implementation as a conceit and justifies the distinction which Gracián at times wishes to make between the *concepto* as a basic idea, and the *agudeza* as the embodiment of such an idea.

We have examined the general principles on which Gracián's theory of wit is based, but not all the intricacies of how the individual chapters of his treatise fit the general scheme. There is a certain arbitrariness, particularly in Part Two, in the allocation of topics to chapters. The erudition displayed by some writers displaying wit which is the topic of Discursos XLVIII and XLIX, for example, in effect serves to remind us that Classical mythology can provide a useful source for conceits but does not on the evidence given by Gracián demonstrate that the use of scholarly references takes us into a theoretically distinct area of wit. As for Discursos LX-LXII, they offer some fascinating judgments on the style of many important writers, but take Gracián well beyond his brief and take us into areas which have no necessary connection with wit. I shall resist the temptation of following Gracián onto the terrain of these *obiter dicta*.

Chapter Two: The rival theorists

A good way of refining our appreciation of the strengths and weaknesses of Gracián's approach to wit is to place it alongside that of other theorists. It is particularly interesting to see instances of disagreements between them on the one hand, and instances of common views arrived at apparently quite independently on the other.

Gracián was not the first theorist, yet in his treatise he talks of the theory of wit as a brand new enterprise and makes no acknowledgment of the previously published work of the Italian Matteo Peregrini, *Delle acutezze* (1636). Peregrini, for his own part, was to indirectly accuse Gracián of plagiarism, a charge we shall investigate later. But there was one theorist, Sarbiewski, whose work pre-dates both of them with which neither the Italian nor the Spaniard could have been expected to be familiar, since it remained unpublished.

. Although his was the first known treatise on wit, Sarbiewski's work is particularly interesting for its critical, questioning approach. His views are already the product of a debate between fellow Jesuit rhetoricians in a number of different countries. Having taught rhetoric at Polotsk between 1618 and 1620, during which period he was developing his theory of wit, Sarbiewski went to study theology in Rome to prepare himself for the priesthood. While there, he was encouraged by friends to lecture on his theory, which he did in the late summer of 1623.[16] It seems that his correspondence with other scholars interested in wit dates from this period, to judge by Denys Petau's response to his request for his view on wit which appears in Petau's published correspondence, and which, although undated in the printed text, is addressed to him at Rome.[17] Sarbiewski then incorporated his response to the views of others into his theory when he gave another course of lectures on wit on returning to teach rhetoric in Polotsk again in 1626. It is through the publication this century of the lecture notes of this course that the modern reader has access to Sarbiewski's theory.[18]

In general Gracián's theory emerges unscathed from the criticisms raised by Sarbiewski. But some views later to be espoused by the Italian theorists and their followers are summarily dismissed by Sarbiewski in convincing fashion. One

---

[16] "Tractatus etiam suos de Acuto et Arguto quos in patria scripserat, poscentibus amicis Romae praelegere per Augustum et Septembrem instituit." T. Wall, *Casimiri Sarbiewski e societate Jesu Poloniae Poemata Omnia* (Staraviesiae, 1892), p. viii. The other biographical details are also taken from Wall.

[17] *Dionysii Petavii Aurelianensis e societ. Iesu epistolarum* (Paris, 1652), p.237.

[18] In *Wykłady poetyki. Praecepta poetica*, ed. Stanislaw Skimina (Warsaw-Krakow, 1958) pp. 1-20, from which I take quotations from Sarbiewski's text.

cannot, he argues, define a conceit as a kind of metaphor, or as a pithy saying, or as a kind of logical fallacy, all views to be taken up by later theorists. In the end he defines wit as a *discordia concors*, a mixture of harmonious and discordant elements.

It is interesting that the very same phrase is used by Samuel Johnson in the following century to describe the wit of the Metaphysical Poets.[19] Despite the fact that he could have had no direct access to Sarbiewski's treatise, there is one route via which he could have known that the Polish scholar had referred to wit as a *discordia concors*. Michael Radau, another Jesuit teacher of rhetoric, in his *Orator extemporaneus* gives a very brief partial account of Sarbiewski's theory of wit. Radau, who was born in Braunsberg in 1617, the year in which Sarbiewski was finishing his philosophical studies there, seems to have had close connections with the Jesuit College at Vilnius, writing an oration in praise of the benefactors of the college.[20] And no doubt it was here, where the first edition of his *Orator extemporaneus* was published, that Radau gained access to Sarbiewski's manuscript. For Sarbiewski had taught rhetoric and then theology there between 1626 and his death in 1640, the very year in which the *Orator extemporaneus* first appeared. This treatise had various editions, one of them in London in 1657, and so it is perfectly plausible that Johnson might have come across it.

One of Sarbiewski's eighteenth-century enthusiasts, Lebrecht Gotthelf Langbein, frustrated at the unavailability of the *De acuto et arguto*, has some harsh words to say about Radau, accusing him of surreptitiously appropriating the manuscript after Sarbiewski's death. Langbein begs the Jesuits at Vilnius to unearth and publish the text in case it happened to be lying forgotten in some corner.[21] But with hindsight one can see that very little of the detail of Sarbiewski's theory is reproduced by Radau. Indeed, he adds his own interpretation of the nature of the *discordia concors*

> Just as physically speaking the point of a triangle is the coming together of two sides into a point and their union derives from a single base, so the metaphorical point is a coming together or a harmonious discord of the subject and predicate in speech. Or to give a briefer definition the acumen is a harmonious discord or a discordant harmony : that is when we speak in a witty way the predicate and subject of speech on the one hand agree with each other, and on the other disagree with each other.[22]

---

19 *Lives of the English Poets*, ed. G.B. Hill (Oxford, Clarendon Press, 1905), 3 vols, Vol. 1, p. 20

20 *Orationes in laudem Befactorum Colegii Vilnensis* (Vilnius, 1640), listed in Backer's *Biblioteque de la Compagnie de Jésus*

21 *Commentatu de Matthiae Casimiri Sarbievii S.I. Poloni vita studiis et scriptis* (Dresdae, Apud Redericum Hekdium, 1754), pp. 76-7.

22 'Sicut materiale Acumen est duarum linearum seu duorum laterum in unum punctum concursus et unio ex uno fundamento provenient: ita Acumen metaphoricum est concursus seu discors concordia Subjecti & Praedicati in oratione. Alii sic brevius definient: Acumen est concors discordia, seu discors concordia: h.e. tunc acute vero parte secum disconveniunt.' *Orator Extemporaneus*, (London, 1657), p.22

The reference to subject and predicate here is Radau's own, and is not found in Sarbiewski.

Johnson's understanding of the *discordia concors* as 'a combination of dissimilar images, or discovery of occult resemblances in things apparently unlike' is quite different from Sarbiewski's. Sarbiewski is at pains to point out that his *discordia concors* does not imply a union of opposites, but rather means that what is said of the matter in hand partly seems to fit, and partly does not.[23]

As for Radau's explanation of the theory, despite Langbein's suspicions, it is far from being a slavish repetition of Sarbiewski's views. For example, in discussing the production of conceits Sarbiewski had limited himself to a general exposition of how the Topics of Invention traditionally used by rhetoricians could be adapted to the discovery of conceits. Radau contents himself with noting that the topics all provide an ample source of wit, and that there is none which cannot be pressed into service.[24] He precedes this with his own list of practical hints of a more linguistically orientated kind for producing a *discordia concors*, such as the introduction by the writer of a discordant epithet, or a second discordant subject, or the use of catachresis, or the simultaneous affirmation and negation of the same thing but in different senses.[25] Such examples could have led some readers, of whom Johnson might have been one, to think primarily in terms of a finding of likeness in the unlike.

Radau further shows his independence by adding an extra twist to the Sarbiewski basic theory when he says that the *discordia concors* pertains between the subject and the predicate in an utterance, whereas Sarbiewski had talked more vaguely, using the Latin term *res* ('the matter'), rather in the same way that Gracián referred to the 'subject of discourse' ('el subjeto sobre quien se discurre'). But the problem with Radau's more grammatical approach is that it makes analysis much more difficult when writers move away from straightforward predication, particularly when they use figurative language. Nevertheless, Radau's desire for precision is laudable, and we ourselves will need to probe more closely what 'the subject' means in Gracián in a later chapter.

There are a number of ways in which the theories of Sarbiewski and Gracián coincide. One detail on which they both agree is that wit involves the particular. Dismissing the idea that a conceit is the same as a *sententia*, a maxim, Sarbiewski argues that maxims are universal and concern everyday matters, whereas wit does not.[26] Gracián puts a slightly different slant on things by admitting some *sentencias*

---

23   'illud dictum ad rem ipsam ex una parte videatur non pertinere, et altera autem videatur valde pertinere.' *De acuto et arguto*, p.6, 1.31

24   'Bonus fons Acuminis redundat primim ex locis Dialecticis, (Definitio, Part. enum. &c) Nullus enim fere tam sterilis est, ex quo, si rem de qua loqueris circumducas, Acumen haurire non possit.' *Op.cit.*, 25.

25   *Op.cit.*, 24

26   'Sententia semper est universale dictum ex quotidiano rerum usu et humana vita extractum: *Audentes Fortuna iuvat*. Acumen contra saepe circa singularem materiam versatur.' *Op.cit.*, 4. I have corrected the misprinted word 'materiem' in this text.

to the fold of wit, but insisting that they have to be specific and not general in nature:

> Las [sentencias] que son propias de esta arte de agudeza, son aquéllas que se sacan de la ocasión y les da pie alguna circunstancia especial, de modo que no son sentencias generales, sino muy especiales, glosando alguna rara contingencia[27]

As far as the basic theory of both writers is concerned, the concept of the *discordia concors* clearly fits very well Gracián's *agudeza de improporción*. As Gracián says of the *agudeza por ponderación de dificultad*, 'a dissonance between the subject and its effect produces an agreeable harmony'.[28]   But what is in doubt is the compatibility of Gracián's *agudeza de proporción* with a theory which insists that there has to be a discordant element in all conceits of whatever type.

The rationale behind Sarbiewski's insistence on the dual nature of wit is explained in his first chapter where he identifies two psychological components in our reaction to a conceit: wonder and pleasure.   But he is keen to see the conceit as having objective qualities which do not depend on the state of mind of the individual reader. The pleasure derives from the remarkable pertinence of the relationship on which the conceit is based, and the wonder, in his view, from its unexpectedness, which is caused by a dissonant element in the conceit.   Sarbiewski rejects the definition of the conceit solicited from Denys Petau as 'quod et praeter communem usum exspectationemque sit, et cum re, qua de agitur, maxime coniunctum' on the grounds that the unexpectedness is an effect rather than a cause. However, it would be easy to get into a sterile chicken/egg argument here, and Petau's definition does provide a degree of objectivity in that the phrase 'praeter communem usum' does not rely on the experiences of individual readers, but talks of what is outside the common run of things.   Basically all these theorists are agreed that what is required in wit is something extraordinary.   Hence Gracián's constant insistence in the course of his treatise that to produce conceits we should always be on the lookout for some special circumstance. But what we need to question is whether it is appropriate to regard this extraordinariness as a negative factor, as something dissonant. On logical grounds this is questionable, since the alleged dissonance would be between our expectations and the outcome revealed in the conceit rather than between the subject of the conceit and its causes, effects, circumstances, etc. On psychological grounds one could also object that as readers, our sense of the remarkable in a conceit is not always felt by us to be something dissonant or negative.   My own experience suggests that the pleasure and the wonder experienced when I enjoy a fine conceit is not easily distinguishable from that felt when have I encountered a remarkable coincidence in my life. In thinking to oneself 'What a remarkable combination of circumstances!' one is not making some comparison between what has happened and something else

---

27 *Op.cit.,* 377
28 'una disonancia entre el sujeto y su efecto hace agradable armonía.' *Op.cit.,* 267

more ordinary which one might have expected to happen. There are infinite number of 'something elses' which might have happened but which simply do not come into the picture.

There is an indication that Sarbiewski himself is aware that some conceits might not quite fit his definition. He attempts to meet the objection in Chapter Six, when he declares that although there are such conceits, these are nearly all cases of verbal wit, and thus not examples of true wit. His grounds for saying this are not explained. He uses the term *argutum* rather than *acutum* to refer to this allegedly inferior wit. This is the least convincing part of Sarbiewski's theory, and we shall return to the issue of verbal wit and its alleged inferiority in the penultimate chapter of this book.

One other theorist who preceded Gracián, and whose treatise was available in print before Gracián wrote his was the Italian Matteo Peregrini. Gracián makes no acknowledgment of Peregrini, and in his introductory remarks to the reader talks of his own theory as something brand new. Peregrini, however, felt aggrieved at what he saw as plagiarism on the Spaniard's part.[29] On the basis of the divergences between both theorists A.A. Parker states baldly that Gracián had not read Peregrini's treatise. Nevertheless, despite fundamental differences in their approach, there is one vital part of Gracián's theory which is also found in Peregrini and in no other theorist. This is the idea that wit consists in a kind of beauty. It is by no means impossible that Gracián derived this idea from Peregrini.

It is in Chapter Three of *Delle acutezze* that Peregrini expounds his argument.[30] The primary materials in wit are words and things, and wit consists in making links between them, links which he takes as a presupposition need to be beautiful — 'l'acutezza per cosa artificiosa e presupposta'. And since this beauty needs to arouse wonder, it needs to be very special — 'grandemente raro'. This special quality is based on revealing a highly harmonious match between the parts of the utterance which have been linked together in a beautiful way — 'far comparire una molta vicendevole acconcezza tra le parti nel detto artificiosamente legate'. Such is the case in music, he states, and there is common agreement that physical beauty depends primarily on proportion — 'una rarità di proporzione'. At this point Peregrini's theory is close to Gracián's. But they soon part company after this.

Peregrini's opinion that beauty was a requirement of wit was later criticized by Sforza Pallavicino in his *Trattato dello stile*. Pallavicino, after making some flattering remarks about Peregrini and expressing regret that he had not read his treatise before composing his own, makes his challenge on a number of grounds. Firstly he argues that the comic displays wit, but that laughter is, as Aristotle had claimed, a reaction to ugliness rather than beauty. Secondly, whereas sight and the

---

[29]   ' ... un certo che, tradotto il mio libretto *Delle acutezze* in castigliano, se ne fece autore', *Trattasti e narratori del seicento,* ed. Ezio Raimondi (Milan-Naples, Ricciardi, 1960), p.173.

[30]   *Trattatisti e narratori del Seicento*, p.118.

imagination delight in beauty, the intellect even though it responds to beauty requires truth rather than beauty to be satisfied. Finally, one can have conceits in which the subject matter is horrifying rather than beautiful. Pallavicino concludes that the sole requirement of wit is novelty rather than a novel beauty.[31]

Pallavicino's objections can be countered in various ways. Even if Aristotle were right and laughter were invariably a response to incongruity, it does not follow that in the case of a comic conceit our response is exhausted by the act of laughing. We could at the same time as we laugh be aware of our enjoyment of an intellectual pattern of a kind which can equally well be found in non-comic conceits. Again, even if we accept the idea that truth is a requirement for intellectual enjoyment, where there is falseness in a conceit it does not follow that our appreciation of such a conceit is not rooted in an awareness of what the true situation is. For example, in the case of witty argument which relies on sophistry, the maximum enjoyment is obtained not by the reader being deceived by such sophistry, but by his recognition that this is just a game which the author is playing in complicity with the reader. The reader is expected to see through the deceit, and enjoy the challenge of discovering just where the flaw in the logic is to be found. As for Pallavicino's final objection, the fact that the subject matter of a conceit may be horrifying does not prevent the patterns which it reveals being beautiful.

There is one aspect of the theory of wit on which Peregrini revises his views when he comes to approach the subject again in a second treatise, *I fonti dell'ingegno* (1650). This new treatise concerns the methods recommended for the production of conceits. Originally Peregrini had suggested the use of the so-called Topics, a traditional checklist of headings which found a place in classical rhetorical theory as an aid to the production of arguments. Sarbiewski had also described a method of using the Topics and then, perhaps under the influence of Peregrini, Gracián. Gracián's approach is slightly informal, and he does not enumerate the whole official list of Topics as found in Cicero, but he does refer to them in an obscure way when he says at the start of Discurso IV, 'Las máximas doctrinales son lo que el nombre dice, cabezas y como fuentes del discurrir'. The context makes it clear that *máximas* cannot mean 'maxims' here, which elsewhere in his treatise are called the *máximas prudenciales,* but can only mean the Topics. Now Peregrini in his second treatise denigrates the use of the Topics as a method of producing conceits, and proposes instead a new checklist of his own. Although Aristotle is not mentioned, Peregrini's new list bears a remarkable similarity to Aristotle's Categories or Predicaments.

Peregrini's change of heart could well have been motivated by a desire to get at Gracián, who could have derived the idea of using the Topics from Peregrini and integrated them more successfully into his method than had the Italian. It could have been a case of sour grapes on Peregrini's part.

---

[31]   *Op.cit.,* 197-9

There are further significant ideas in the third chapter of Peregrini's *Delle acutezze* which link up with Tesauro's later theory rather than with Gracián. In discussing the kinds of link which wit makes, Peregrini argues that figurative language in particular produces a beautiful link between words and things. Not only that, but a trope tacitly links the thing literally referred to and that figuratively referred to. The tacit nature of this process makes it akin to the enthymeme, a form of deductive argument in which, unlike in a formal syllogism, part of the reasoning is suppressed but is to be understood.[32]

Peregrini's insight into the nature of metaphor here offers a valuable antidote to the traditional classical view of metaphor as being a question of style rather than of substance. It would have enabled the easy integration of metaphor and other forms of trope into a theory of wit based on logical correspondences. But he fails to capitalize on his discovery, and predominantly views wit as coming within the province of rhetoric rather than logic, and does not distance himself from the traditional view that trope is a more beautiful way of saying what could less colourfully have been put in literal terms.

In his *Cannocchiale Aristotelico* Tesauro followed Peregrini in giving metaphor a prominent role in wit, stating that although not all rhetorical figures show wit, all wit involves figurative language. Tesauro also acknowledges the importance of suppressed logic in the conceit by defining the true conceit as 'an urbanely fallacious enthymeme'. There is a new element here — that of fallaciousness — but the basic idea could have been derived from Peregrini.

Poor Peregrini never received the credit due to him for some fruitful ideas which he himself never developed adequately. Tesauro achieved greater recognition, and, for example, was not only admired but slavishly followed by his Portuguese follower, Leitão Ferreira.[33]

Tesauro seems more or less to take it for granted that all conceits involve figurative language. The nearest he comes to arguing a case for this is when he states that wit consists in the linking of remote and distinct objects, and that this is precisely the role of trope.[34] The obvious fallacy in this argument is that just because trope may achieve this it does not follow that literal language is incapable of doing so. But Tesauro is wedded to the idea of conceits being necessarily

---

[32]   'Il legamento artificoso delle parole con le cose accade ogni volta che la voce o la locuzione sia giudiciosamente trasportata dal suo nativo significato ad un alieno. In questo caso vengono tacitamente ancora legate cose con cose, perche la cosa nuovamente significata viene tacitamente a legarse con quella che nativamente suole significarsi, no sole per la voce fatta comune, ma inseme per quella ragione che ha fatto luogo a simile comunanza.' *Trattatisti e narratori del Seicento*, p. 120.

[33]   See below, n. 54.

[34]   'Se l'ingegno consiste (come dicemo) nel ligare insieme le remote & separate notioni degli propositi obieti: questo apunto e l'officio della Metafora, & non di alcun'altra figura. Et per consequenza ell'e fra le Figure le piu Acuta.' *Trattatisti e narratori del Seicento*, p. 73

metaphorical. He envisages a hierarchy of conceits, starting with one-word metaphors, moving on to metaphorical propositions, and culminating in ingenious arguments. But there are many problems with his scheme, as we shall see.

One difficulty is the need to distinguish between a trope which does display wit and one that does not. He observes that the less superficial and general and the more remote and specific the ideas on which a metaphor is based are, the more wit there will be. As we shall see in a later chapter, remoteness is very hard to quantify with any objectivity. However the requirement of specificity is something on which both Gracián and Sarbiewski agree. The corollary of these observations is that general and obvious metaphors show less wit, arguably no wit at all. Hence it cannot be metaphoricity which characterizes wit.

Another weakness is the attempt to distinguish between the metaphor as a single word and the metaphorical proposition. Single-word metaphors are only recognizable as such because they form part of whole utterances, thus the single word is hardly a viable unit. Again, the relationship between metaphorical propositions and urbanely fallacious enthymemes is unclear. What counts as urbanity? Mere jocular intention? In the interests of consistency, Tesauro is committed to the view that urbanely fallacious enthymemes are based on trope, and therefore, presumably, comprise figurative propositions. But it is not hard to think of examples of witty arguments which do not rely on trope. We shall meet some in the next chapter. Ultimately, Sarbiewski's rejection of the theory that a conceit is a kind of metaphor on the grounds that there are plenty of examples of non-metaphorical wit is unanswerable. And although he was tempted by the theory that a conceit was a kind of fallacious argument, Sarbiewski rejected that too.

Despite his shortcomings Tesauro makes some interesting contributions to the theory of wit. One of these is the analysis of the faculty of wit as dual in nature, consisting of on the one hand an investigative side, perspicacity, and on the other a manipulative side, versatility.[35] This gives wit a quasi scientific role as well as an artistic one and suggests that it is based on an investigation of the real world. Another strengthening of the idea that wit has a cognitive function is Tesauro's claim that conceits are produced not only by man, but also by God and by Nature. Hence the human artist in producing conceits may be seen as reading conceits produced by Nature.

Tesauro's analysis of paradoxical conceits of a particular type in which pairs of contradictories are counterbalanced, which constitute what he calls 'il mirabile', the marvellous, is of particular interest for its applicability to some typical images of Góngora, which Gracián recognized as a speciality of our poet.[36]

---

[35]   *Op. cit.*, 32.
[36]   See *Trattatisti e narratori del Seicento*, pp. 90-94. Gracián says of Góngora 'Fue ...en toda especie de agudeza eminente, pero en ésta de contraproporciones consistió el triunfo de su grande ingenio' *op.cit.*, 254

All in all, Tesauro's obsession with trying to find all the elements of his theory in Aristotle's *Rhetoric*, which on his own admission is the lens through which he contemplates wit, prevents him from achieving sufficient critical detachment to arrive at a viable over all theory.

Not all writers on wit in the seventeenth and eighteenth centuries were striving for a comprehensive theory of wit of their own. For example, Father Dominique Bouhours' treatise, *De la manière de bien penser dans les ouvrages d'esprit*, is largely negative in its thrust, aiming in its informally structured dialogue to protect the French against aping what he sees as the excesses of Spanish and Italian literature in the name of 'le bon sens'. But even if he does not offer a basic theory of his own, his reaction to the ideas of others is interesting, and shows some critical acumen.

Bouhours offers no detailed response to Gracián, largely because he found him incomprehensible. The *Agudeza y arte de ingenio* is described by him as a fine project, badly executed, although it does contain subtlety and sound reason.[37] He found Gracián's basic theory too obscure and too metaphysical. But Bouhours does offer some interesting views on the topic of the true and the false in wit which he relates to Tesauro's theory, and which we in turn might relate to Pallavicino's comment on the intellect's need for truth.

Philanthe, the junior of the two interlocutor's in Bouhours' dialogue, speculates that the main appeal of wit may lie in the false, and that epigrams tend to turn on fiction, double meanings, and hyperbole. Philanthe's companion, Eudoxe, comments that fiction is not the same as falseness, and that fictions may display verisimilitude and may hide truths. Philanthe amplifies his point by noting that Aristotle reduced wit to metaphor, which is a kind of trickery, and that Tesauro saw the subtlest thoughts as a kind of figurative enthymeme. Eudoxe replies that 'le figuré n'est pas faux, & la metaphore a sa verité aussi-bien que la fiction'. He goes on to comment that only the crudest of readers would take metaphorical ideas literally, and that in that respect they fool nobody. The point is echoed later by Muratori, who is every bit as cautious as Bouhours in accepting literary conceits.[38]

If Bouhours accepts in principle that metaphor can have a valuable cognitive function, he is less complimentary about punning which may offer truth in its figurative sense but falseness in its literal sense. The issue of how far verbal wit can legitimately be regarded as inferior is one we shall take up in Chapter Six. It is one of the main issues which emerges from Joseph Addison's theory expounded in his series of six articles published in the Spectator in 1711. Addison talks initially as if he is unaware of previous theories of wit. But eventually he owns up to admiring Bouhours, which may explain his preoccupation with what distinguishes true from false wit.

---

37 *La manière de bien penser dans les ouvrages d'esprit* (Paris 1987), p.364
38 He says of 'imagine fantastiche ben fatte' that 'la lor falsità significa il vero' L.A. Muratori, *Della perfetta poesia Italiana*, ed. A.M. Salvini (Milan, 1821), Vol I, p. 274.

It is amusing to put Bouhours' fairly kindly comments about the role of metaphor alongside his strictures about hyperbole in which moderation is required to rule. If, as Bouhours argues, one would have to be very stupid to take metaphor literally and consequently object to its false nature, the same ought to apply to hyperbole which is but another form of trope, which, like metaphor, needs to be taken with a pinch of salt. But as we shall see in Chapter Six hyperbole is one of the most difficult tropes to analyse adequately, so perhaps Bouhours' inconsistency is understandable.

Another theorist who reacts to Gracián's treatise is the Portuguese Leitão Ferreira, who on his own admission basically follows Tesauro's theory.[39] What distinguishes the Portuguese theorist is the detailed interest he takes in expounding the philosophical exposition of mental activities. He criticises Gracián for his famous definition of the *concepto* in apparently purely mental terms as 'un acto del entendimiento que exprime la correspondencia que se halla entre los objectos' on the grounds that it fails to refer to the conceit as a verbally manifested physical entity. Clearly this means that *exprime* was not interpreted by Leitão Ferreira as meaning 'express in words'. But if it was Gracián's intention to make a clear distinction between the *concepto* as a mental entity, and the *agudeza* as the outward physical representation of it then it is hard to see the force of Leitão's argument. Ironically enough it is Leitão himself who can be said to waste space on irrelevant definitions when he defines a concept, 'o concepto, nao engenhoso, mas simple'. Definitions of non-witty concepts ought to have no place in a theory of wit.

Occasionally the trail of references to other writers on wit by the theorists leads to some rather obscure sources and is an indication of the extraordinary wealth of contributions on the subject over the space of a century. But the chances of there being some undiscovered masterpiece on the subject are probably slim. Leitão Ferreira includes on his list Juglaris, Garifalo, and Masen. Masen's name also crops up in another treatise on wit by D. G. Morhof. One of Sarbiewski's biographers, Lebrecht Gotthelf Langbein, relays the rumour that Sarbiewski's treatise on wit had been divulged in detail by Michael Radau to Morhof, also a fellow Jesuit. Morhof himself, however, makes no mention of Sarbiewski, but admits a debt to Masen, Tesauro, Mercerius, and Carolus a St Antonio. Certainly the debt to Tesauro is plain to see in the use of an *index categoricus*. What might these writers have learned from Jacob Masen's *Ars nova argutiarum* (1649)? Masen's general description of an *argutia* as 'a conclusion or pithy saying [sententia] which is unexpected or contrary to expectation'[40] shows a workmanlike but unsubtle approach. He goes on to enumerate a series of methods of producing the unexpected. The general approach offers nothing which cannot be found in Pallavicino's eminently practical theory,

---

[39]   'Seguirey as doutrinas do Conde Gran Cruz Manuel Tesauro', Francisco Leitão Ferreira, *Nova arte de conceitos*, (Lisbon, Antonio Pedrozo Cebran, 1718, 1721) 2 vols, Vol I, p.7. He also goes on to acknowledge other theorists. See Mercedes Blanco, *Les rhétoriques de la Pointe*, Paris 1992, p. 426, n.3

[40]   'praeter aut contra expectationem allata, vel conclusio, vel sententia', p. 10.

which defines the conceit as 'una osservazione maravigliosa raccolta in un detto breve'[41], and goes on to specify a series of techniques for producing wonder. At the general level, however, neither Masen nor Pallavicino offers an acceptable theory. An analysis of what is wrong with their definitions can serve to bring out the advantages of Gracián's general theory above all others.

Firstly, Masen's definition is too narrow in specifying that only conclusions and *sententiae* qualify as conceits. There are numerous examples to be found in Góngora of non sententious utterances which could not be described as conclusions either, but whose wit is manifest. Pallavicino's more general word 'una osservazione', an observation, still fails to include instances of wit which find expression other than in words. Gracián wisely leaves open the medium of expression for conceits and sees them simply as the results of an act of the understanding.

The requirement that a witty utterance should be marvellous or unexpected though probably sound is of relatively little use in the absence of a more specific account of what exactly we are responding to in a conceit. An account of Christ's miracles might seem marvellous, but could be totally lacking in wit. If somebody tells me that my shoelace is undone or that I have won the football pools, this would be surprising to me, but probably devoid of wit. Peregrini and Gracián supply the vital ingredient in specifying that it is the making of connections between elements which characterises wit which reveal how they match or correspond. The nature of these correspondences may inspire wonder or surprise, but there are some dangers in making such responses part of the definition. Although I may admire even more greatly a conceit of Góngora's on reading it for the umpteenth time, clearly in one sense I am not any longer surprised by it. One can, like Petau, offer a more objective test by appealing to a collective sense of what is surprising or not. Ideally it is better to refine the account of what it is we are responding to rather than stressing the nature of the response.

Beauty and subtlety are the features latched onto by Gracián. But Gracián develops his account of the aesthetic nature of correspondences in a different way from Peregrini. Peregrini's manouevre which gets him from the idea of beauty to the need to use figurative language in the conceit is based on the belief that it is the way that the connections are made that is beautiful rather than the nature of the connections themselves. This fits the traditional view of trope as a more colourful way of expressing things which could have been put more plainly in literal language. Gracián, however, is far less interested in diction and sees the beauty of wit as inherent in the correspondences themselves independently of how they may be expressed. He also makes it clear that the correspondences of wit should be seen as operating at a more abstract level than purely physical correspondences. If my tie matches my shirt that may constitute a beautiful correspondence, but it lacks the

---

41   *Trattatisti e narratori del Seicento*, p. 201

abstract logical content, the rationality, which would make the match in question appeal to the intellect.

To round off my account of how the various theorists of wit relate to each other I shall consider the general theoretical approach of twentieth-century critics towards wit and how it relates to earlier theories.

Those approaching wit with a background in English studies typically with no acquaintance with the European theorists have found no shortage of pronouncements on wit in seventeenth- and eighteenth-century England. George Williamson's *The Proper Wit of Poetry*[42] is rich in examples, but ultimately the lack of any clear underlying basic theory can make it difficult to see the wood for the trees. One idea specific to England is the connection made between wit and 'fancy', a term whose sense seems to have changed to some extent,[43] but which insofar as it implies liveliness of invention fails as an exclusive criterion for wit because it ignores the intellectual quality which distinguishes whit from mere whimsy.

English scholars interested in the Metaphysical poets have inevitably given prominence to Samuel Johnson's characterization of wit as 'a combination of dissimilar images, or discovery of occult resemblances in things apparently unlike'. It is this definition which is at the root of Helen Gardner's account of the conceit when she says that

> All comparisons disclose likeness in things unlike: a comparison
> becomes a conceit when we are made to concede likeness while being
> strongly aware of unlikeness[44]

This idea that all wit is based on the relationship of similarity is nowhere to be found in the Spanish or Italian theorists or in Sarbiewski, for all of whom, quite rightly in my view, similarity is but one of a range of possible relationships behind wit. But English speaking hispanists who have written on the theory of wit seem to have allowed the Johnsonian approach to colour their interpretation of the seventeenth-century treatises. Thus Edward Sarmiento, the pioneer in the field, talks in terms of objects placed in juxtaposition and 'shown in their different aspects to be similar or dissimilar'.[45] And Terence May, who criticised Sarmiento's preoccupation with metaphor as a basis for the conceit, also seems to have assumed, although he is far too subtle to be caught saying it directly, that *correspondencia* is tantamount to similarity. Without this assumption May's insistence that the *agudeza de semejanza* is problematic for Gracián makes no sense. And A.A. Parker, who sees conceits as based on metaphor, the trope of resemblance, by the same token gives similarity a key role in wit. Robert Pring-Mill, whilst being critical of aspects of Parker's

---

42   (London, Faber, 1961)
43   See R. B. Martin, *The Triumph of Wit. A Study of Victorian Comic Theory.* (Oxford, Clarendon Press, 1974), p. 33.
44   See her introduction to *The Metaphysical Poets* (Oxford, Clarendon Press, 1961)
45   'Gracián's Agudeza y arte de ingenio', *Modern Language Review*, 27, (1932), pp. 280-292 and 420-429 (p. 285)

theory, nails his colours firmly to the mast by citing approvingly Helen Gardner's definition of the conceit[46]

Pring-Mill also has a pat on the head for Sarbiewski, who saw an element of discord as fundamental to wit. And again it seems that Sarmiento, who talks of false analogy in the conceit, and May, who in his latest article on wit talks of a discordant note even in Gracián's *agudeza de proporción*[47] are of like mind. Yet Gracián himself, who places emphasis on beauty, makes no such requirement for a discordant note. Again, I side with Gracián on the grounds that some of my favourite conceits seem to me to show no mismatch at all. One example must suffice here. In the first *Soledad* Góngora says of the first ship to sail the seas:

> Más armas introdujo este marino
> monstruo, escamado de robustas hayas,
> a las que tanto mar divide playas,
> que confusión y fuego
> al frigio muro el otro leño griego. (I, 374-8)

Here the metaphor of the ship as a sea monster with wooden scales enhances the basic analogy between the ship and the Trojan Horse, but is not central to it. The conceit would still have worked if Góngora had simply referred to 'este navío' instead of 'este marino monstruo...'. The axis of the conceit is the word 'leño' — a piece of wood — which links the Trojan Horse to the ship via what we might identify as a synecdoche, although the sense of this word being figurative is not strong, since literally both horse and ship are wooden vessels. What is impressive here is the particularity of the parallel, meeting Gracián's requirement of a 'circunstancia especial', and the perfection of the match between these two treacherous transporters of warriors. Góngora adds to the pleasure with a modicum of subtlety by alluding to rather than naming the horse. Where, I ask, is the mismatch which Sarbiewski and my Hispanist colleagues would have me see in such a conceit? I am not aware of having been forced to concede likeness whilst being strongly aware of unlikeness.

Another common feature of the critics mentioned thus far, with the exception of May, is the view that conceits are essentially metaphorical. Not even Tesauro was this restrictive, since by *metafora* he means not specifically metaphor, the trope of resemblance, but trope of all kinds, including metonymy, hyperbole, etc. Here I side with Sarbiewski in claiming that there are conceits which do not involve metaphor or, indeed, any kind of trope.

Hugh H. Grady has also indicated that Gracián's theory does not support the idea that conceits are necessarily metaphorical or involve a *discordia concors*, arguing, as I myself demonstrated in 1968,[48] that Gracián's terminology derives from the theory of

---

[46]   R. D. F. Pring-Mill, '"Porque yo cerca muriese". An occasional meditation on a conceptista theme', *Bulletin of Hispanic Studies*, 61 (1984), pp. 369-78

[47]   'Notes on Gracián's "agudeza"', in *Wit of the Golden Age*, *Op.cit.*, 270-283 (p. 282)

[48]   'Gracián, Peregrini and the theory of Topics', *Modern Language Review*, 58 (1968), pp. 854-863.

Topics. He does however seem to misrepresent May's views, and also confuses things by using the word 'commonplace' ambiguously, stating that 'wit works within the commonplace subject-adjacents relation to discover additional, noncommonplace relations among them to form the conceit of proportion'.[49] The relationships Gracián relies on are all to be found on the standard list of Topics or 'commonplaces'. Extraordinary as the conceit may be, in logical terms it is constructed from perfectly standard elements.

Amongst the Spaniards themselves Gracián's theory has attracted little detailed scrutiny. Emilio Hidalgo-Serna's *El pensamiento ingenioso en Baltasar Gracián. El "concepto" y su función lógica*,[50] has an axe to grind about the cognitive value of wit, emphasising the importance of the *agudeza de perspicacia*, which is not properly described by Gracián, and on his own admission plays no part in his treatise. Hidalgo-Serna also draws on material of dubious relevance to wit from *El Criticón* and *El Discreto* while neglecting important issues raised by the text of Gracián's *Agudeza*. Antonio Carreira's anthology of Góngora's poetry shows a welcome appreciation of Góngora's wit in its preface, focussing especially on techniques of verbal wit in Góngora. But Carreira's reading of Gracián's treatise seems a little skimpy, failing to identify accurately four basic types of conceit, and introducing the idea of false analogy which does not appear in Gracián's text.

It has been left to the French to produce the first comprehensive detailed study of the European theories of wit with Mercedes Blanco's impressive book, *Les rhétoriques de la pointe. Baltasar Gracián et le conceptisme en Europe*.[51] She stresses Gracián's awareness of the great variety of wit, and in her account of his theory shows herself to be aware that *correspondencia* encompasses a range of relationships other than likeness and unlikeness. But she too is tempted into adding features not directly specified by Gracián thereby reducing his flexibility. Thus Gracián's basic *agudeza de proporción* is accounted for in these terms:

> Suivant le point de vue qu'on décide d'adopter, cette sorte de pointe peut être décrite de plusieurs manières. En termes rhétoriques elle revient au couplage d'un lien de contiguïté (relations de causes à effet, d'événement à circonstances etc..) et d'un lien de similitude, ou pour le dire autrement, à l'association d'une métonymie et d'une métaphore qui joueraient simultanément entre deux termes. On pourrait l'envisager également comme un effet de surdétermination portant sur un récit réel ou virtuel, ou comme un commentaire que vient se greffer sur la ligne narrative, en

---

49   Hugh H. Grady, 'Rhetoric wit and art in Gracián's Agudeza', *Modern Language Quarterly*, 41 (1980), pp. 21-37 (p. 24)
50   Translated from German by Manuel Canet (Barcelona, Anthropos, 1993)
51   Mercedes Blanco, *Les rhétoriques de la pointe.* Baltasar Gracián et le conceptisme en Europe (Paris, Champion, 1992)

introduisant dans se failles, au dessus de l'enchainement temporel ou
causal, des relations supplémentaires, une sorte de saturation logique[52]

The idea of a kind of logical overkill is an interesting and fruitful one. It is also
true, as we shall see, that some of Góngora's conceits involve a combination of
metonymy and metaphor. But the complexity of multiple relationships is not a
requirement stipulated by Gracián any more than is the use of trope, and such
complexity is I believe absent from some of Góngora's conceits. Witness Góngora's
witty pretence in his sonnet 'Oh Claro honor del líquido elemento' (Millé 220) that
the reflection of his beloved is being borne downstream to the sea,[53] or his play on
the word 'bestias' in his Sonnet 'Grandes, más que elefantes' (Millé 252) in order to
refer to the courtiers in their coaches drawn by fellow beasts, the horses.[54]

And so we come to the application of the theory of wit to Góngora's practice. A
prominent factor in Gracián's mind when he produced his theory was the virtuosity of
the poetry of Góngora from which he draws so many of his illustrations. Gracián
recognized the sheer range of Góngora's wit but saw him as having a particular talent
for the 'agudeza de contraposición'. From the modern reader's point of view, the
disappointing thing about Gracián's handling of his examples from Góngora is firstly
that so many of the poet's most impressive conceits are omitted in favour of what
often seem less exciting cases. Secondly, though less surprisingly, such practical
analysis as there is rather skimpy and generally fails to do justice to the sheer
complexity of the process of reading Góngora.

My analysis of Góngora's use of wit in later chapters, might at first glance seem
to be following an agenda laid down by Tesauro with Góngora's use of trope and of
fallacious argument figuring prominently. But this would be a misleading
impression. Trope, which Gracián acknowledged as an important medium for wit, is
given pride of place here because it figures so prominently in Góngora's work. It
takes centre stage for practical rather than theoretical reasons. The use of trope
happens to be an elegant way of helping to meet Gracián's requirement that wit
should be subtle in that the relationships underlying tropes are implicit rather than
explicit. There is an analogy here with the use of allusion as a source of wit which,
as Mercedes Blanco has interestingly argued, was prized by Gracián, but poses special
theoretical difficulties.[55]

Against the background of Gracián's general theory, my aim in commenting on
specific conceits is to draw on relevant material from any of the theorists where it
seems illuminating, and to explore the psychology of the reading process in a more
detailed way than was envisaged by the critics from previous centuries.

---

52   *Op.cit.*, 256
53   For a discussion of this poem, see below, p. 85
54   See below p. 112
55   *Op.cit.*, 311-12

Chapter Three: Trope and the literal base

In Chapters Four and Five I shall be examining the very special contribution of Góngora's use of trope to the wit of his poetry. Before doing so I offer in this chapter a general theoretical framework for the understanding of the nature of trope and how it contrasts with literal language. One reason why this is important is that Góngora sometimes operates on the boundaries between the literal and the figurative. The examples I choose are often of a kind which enthusiasts of deconstruction might seize on as welcome examples of the undecidabilities of language. My own view, however, is that the complexities of Góngora's poetic practice in no way undermine the basic principle that there is such a thing as literal language and that figurative language can be defined in relation to it.

First, then, a definition of trope. Trope is not, as is sometimes supposed, a question of the substitution of one word for another, for as Góngora's poetry demonstrates very clearly, particularly in cases of compound trope, there is often no 'original' literal term available for which the alleged substitution could have been made.[56] Trope is probably best thought of as a deviation from perceived linguistic norms — a semantic deviation, in fact. It is a deviation not in the sense that the writer has avoided the use of some literal expression in favour of some other expression, but in that he has used an expression in a way we recognize as non-standard. We recognize this when we realize that the standard interpretation of the writer's words fails to make sense.

Seen from the most general perspective, trope is merely one of a number of possible linguistic deviations. Others include hyperbaton, a deviation from standard word-order, the use of neologisms, an instance of lexical deviation, ellipsis, a divergence from standards of completeness. Góngora's own mimicking of the so-called Greek accusative provides an example of syntactic deviation. One could extend the list to include cockney rhyming slang, which is an interesting case of substitution according to certain rules, or perhaps even typographical errors.

The unbridled use of any of these types of deviation could result ultimately in irredeemable nonsense. For example, hyperbaton which consisted in a completely random shuffling of the words in a sentence would probably not be recognisable as a case of deviation from an understandable word-order. And a sentence in which every word had been suppressed would not seem like an example of ellipsis. Trope, like other forms of deviation, can function as such because it is set in a context which enables the reader to see what linguistic manoeuvres need to be performed to produce a

---

56   For a criticism of the substitution theory of metaphor see Max Black, *Models and Metaphors* (Ithaca, New York,1962), p.25 ff.

meaningful interpretation and to make sense out of what, when read literally, is a kind of nonsense.

Idioms, like tropes, are semantically deviant in that the individual words which make them up are not susceptible to literal interpretation, but unlike tropes they are processed as a whole as standard set phrases whose inner workings do not concern us.

The various individual types of trope are classifiable according to the type of deviation they involve, as examined in Chapter Four. But first it is necessary to justify the very idea that there is such a thing as a standard from which trope can be said to deviate. There is a discernible tradition of radical linguistic scepticism which challenges the whole attempt to separate literal from figurative language on the grounds that what is commonly thought of as literal language is shown on closer analysis to be subject to the workings of metaphor. Friedrich Nietzsche, whose views were developed when he prepared a course on rhetoric at the University of Basel in 1872-3, reached the dramatic conclusion that :

> No such thing as an unrhetorical, "natural" language exists that could be used as a point of reference: language is itself the result of purely rhetorical tricks and devices... Tropes are not something that can be added or subtracted from language at will; they are its truest nature. There is no such thing as a proper meaning that can be communicated only in certain particular cases.[57]

Again, writing of metaphor in his *Philosophy of Rhetoric*, I. A. Richards sharply criticises the assumption that metaphor is "something special and exceptional in the use of language, a deviation from its normal mode of working, instead of the omnipresent principle of all its free action."[58] Placing the emphasis on metaphor as a thought process, he writes, "When we use a metaphor we have two thoughts of different things active together and supported by a single word, or phrase, whose meaning is a result of their interaction,"[59] adding later that "thought is metaphoric, and proceeds by comparison, and the metaphors of language derive therefrom."[60]

Such theories have also found favour in deconstructive criticism, and are espoused by Paul de Man, for example, in his *Allegories of reading*. In general, the post-structuralist critics raise the level of scepticism directed at the idea that there are firm standards in language. Fundamental in all this is the acceptance of Saussure's view of language as a differential system, an idea which Jacques Derrida extends further in his theory of 'la différance', which adds to the concept of difference that of permanent deferral and absence which is further designed to raise general doubts about the security of any semantic analysis. In negative terms, it portrays the attempt to

---

57   As quoted by Paul de Man, *Allegories of Reading* (New Haven-London, Yale University Press, 1979), pp. 105-6

58   I.A. Richards, *The Philosophy of Rhetoric* (Oxford, Oxford University Press, 1978), p. 90

59   *Op.cit.*, 93

60   *Op.cit.*, 94

establish a literal base to language as a vain attempt to appeal to some kind of natural or original meaning as being 'fully present'. But there are also further points added by Derrida to the agenda. For example, he discusses what he sees as the impossibility of philosophy being able to rid itself of metaphor or to account for it in a non-regressive way, discussing the theory expounded by Hegel in his *Aesthetics* of how abstract terms develop from originally sensuous terms through a process of initial metaphorization and subsequent loss of the sensuous meaning through habitual use.[61]   I shall deal with these more recent points first before offering a critique of Saussure's theory which seems to have had far too long a run for its money.

The theory that figurative language is a deviation from literal language does not require us to conceive of literal language as somehow more 'natural' or even as less complex than trope. It does not require us to see literal language as anything other than arbitrary and susceptible to constant change. It does not entail the hankering after some alleged 'fully present' meaning. In any case, the idea of presence or absence in this context makes little sense. The use to which we put a tool is neither present nor absent from that tool, and the same goes for the use of words. The literal interpretation of a word is merely the default interpretation, possibly a temporary one, established by sheer habit, from which we deviate when the context requires us to do so. A large number of words in a language have more than one standard literal use, but the selection of an appropriate literal meaning from the various options is not a process of deviation from a conventional standard, as is the case with trope. If no deviation is required then there is no active trope, although at some stage in the past history of a language some of the literal uses of a word may have derived from the lexicalisation of what was previously perceived as trope.

The linguistic experience of the individual will determine where exactly the line between literal and figurative is drawn. To an inexperienced learner of a language some expressions will be interpreted as tropes which more experienced users will see as literal. Similarly, an experienced reader of Góngora will perhaps process as lexicalisations some instances of metaphor which the poet uses particularly frequently. It is important to note that in both cases, the identification of what is referred to by the expressions in question will be the same for both experienced and inexperienced readers. What may be affected is the reader's perception of the linguistic adventurousness of the writer.

Whether or not it is the case, as Derrida claims, that philosophers in the main strive to eliminate metaphorical language from their writings but fail miserably, the presence of trope in these circumstances in no way undermines the attempt to distinguish between literal and figurative language. A philosopher exploring difficult terrain may well be handicapped by the lack of a convenient literal terminology. If in

---

61   See his essay 'White mythology' in *Margins of Philsophy*, translated by Alan Bass (New York, London, etc, 1982), p.207 ff.

the circumstances he finds it convenient or necessary to use tropes, our sense of the difference between literal and figurative language, far from being weakened by this, will actually be reinforced. We will note the gap between the way the terms used by the philosopher are normally used, and they new way in which he now uses them, an awareness of which would have been totally absent had he used a purely literal mode of expression.

Derrida's contention that there is a circularity in the philosophy of metaphor which entails at its root the whole phenomenon of conceptualisation is open to the objection that all language, literal or figurative, presupposes the ability to conceptualise. The interpretation of nouns being used literally to refer to physical objects does indeed require the ability to classify objects. But this is a biological gift enjoyed not only by the users of languages, but by insects in recognizing their mates, their food, and, if they are lucky, their predators. As for I.A. Richards' claim that thought is metaphoric, one can object that the perception of an analogy is not itself metaphorical any more than an ability to count is synecdochic. These are simply mental skills necessary for processing any kind of language, literal or figurative.

At a more general level, the whole idea that language has a secure literal base is challenged by the basic Saussurean view accepted by Derrida and his followers that the elements in a linguistic system owe their identity solely to the way in which they mutually interrelate rather than to any features they have in their own right. As Saussure sees it, in a language things are what they are purely by virtue of not being what they are not, and not because they have any positive identity.

> Dans la langue il n'y a que des différences. Bien plus, une différence suppose en général des termes positifs entre lesquels elle s'établit; mais dans la langue il n'y a que des différences sans termes positifs.[62]

The effect of the acceptance of this view, which plays a key role in structuralist and post-structuralist literary theory, is to portray literal language as scarcely any different from metaphorical language and as possibly more complex in that it would seem to involve an interaction between a vast multiplicity of elements instead of one between just two terms. Thus the baldest of utterances brings the entire linguistic system into play.

The primacy of the total system in Saussurean theory leads to some serious difficulties when it comes to accounting for the practical operation of a language. The problems relate mainly to how a language can originate, how it can change, and how it can be acquired by the individual user. What mechanism can there be for any interaction between the system in its totality and the individual user?

Jacques Derrida, commenting on the problem of relating the speech of the individual to the linguistic system , writes:

---

62   F. de Saussure, *Cours de linguistique générale,* ed. Tullio de Mauro (Paris, Payot, 1984), p. 166

We can extend to the system of signs in general what Saussure says about language: "The linguistic system (*langue*) is necessary for speech events (*parole*) to be intelligible and produce there effects, but the latter are necessary for the system to establish itself..." There is a circle here, for if one distinguishes rigourously *langue* and *parole*, code and message, schema and usage, etc. and if one is to do justice to the two principles here enunciated, one does not know where to begin and how something can in general begin, be it *langue* or *parole*. One must therefore recognize, prior to any dissociation of *langue* and *parole*, code and message, and what goes with it, a systematic production of differences, the *production* of a system of differences — a *différance* among whose effects one might later, by abstraction and for specific reasons, distinguish a linguistics of *langue* from a linguistics of *parole*.[63]

Derrida's analysis does nothing to explain 'how something in general can begin,' and in fact creates one or two additional problems of its own. Giving the initial process a name, *la différance*, does not explain the mystery of how it might come about, and to what extent there is any human intervention in the process. And even if we accept the proposition that a language is initially produced by some opaque process, we still have the problem of explaining how once the system has been set up and is in use a new user can acquire a working knowledge of the system. Moreover, Derrida's presumed system of differences envisaged as encompassing both *langue* and *parole* makes little sense in Saussurean terms, since for Saussure *la langue* itself is the differential system on which *la parole* is based. The two are not of the same order, *la parole* is already encompassed by *la langue*.

Merleau-Ponty makes a brave attempt to account in Saussurean terms for the process of language acquisition and linguistic change in his book *Signs*.

Language is learned, and in this sense one is certainly obliged to go from part to whole. The prior whole which Saussure is talking about cannot be the explicit and articulated whole of complete language as it is recorded in grammars and dictionaries. Nor does he have in mind a logical totality like that of a philosophical system, all of whose elements can (in principle) be deduced from a single idea. Since what he is doing is rejecting any other than a "diacritical" meaning of signs, he cannot base language upon a system of positive ideas. The unity he is talking about is a unity of coexistence, like that of the sections of an arch which shoulder one another.

In a unified whole of this kind, the learned parts of a language have an immediate value as a whole, and progress is made less by addition and juxtaposition than by the internal articulation of a function which is its

---

63   As quoted by Jonathan Culler, *On Deconstruction* (London, Routledge & Kegan Paul, 1983), pp. 96-7

own way already complete ... a language sometimes remains a long time pregnant with transformations which are to come; and the enumeration of the means of expression in a language does not have any meaning, since those which fall into disuse continue to lead a diminished life in the language and since the place of those which are to replace them is sometimes already marked out--even if only in the form of a gap, a need, or a tendency.[64]

From this description there emerges no unequivocal explanation of what is supposed to happen every time we learn a new word, for example.   Two, and possibly three, different and incompatible models of how the whole and the parts relate to each other in a language seem to be vying with each other in Merleau-Ponty's account.

The first model is of a whole which comprises the learned parts of the language and those parts alone. That is, they have a value as a whole, as opposed to within a larger whole. But, as Merleau-Ponty observes, in Saussurean terms, such a totality is not built up by the addition or juxtaposition of parts. It follows that every time we learn a new word, instead of expanding the previous whole by a simple addition we would have to construct an entire new system. It would be hard to imagine a more inefficient procedure. It amounts to a denial of the possibility of learning by experience, because we would constantly have to be going back to Square One, knocking down the arch and building a new one every time we are presented with a new stone.

A second model of how whole and parts relate is that of a whole which incorporates the learned parts of the language, but reserves space, as it were, for future developments. But how can I possibly know how many gaps to leave, and where, for the words I have not yet encountered , and may well never encounter?

Indeed the very idea that there could be a specific number of gaps is illusory. It is both physically and theoretically impossible to ascertain, for example, how many words there are in the English language at present. Where the limits of a language lie is a matter not of fact but of opinion. What possible mechanism could there be for determining exactly when a word becomes obsolete, or when a neologism becomes incorporated into the language?

This second model presents an essentially magical theory of language, in which absent experiences exert an inexplicable force, just as in Derrida we have a strange world of invisible writing, signs which efface themselves, a world of shadowy traces at play, all at the wave of the magic wand of *la différance*. It is also magic because Merleau-Ponty's arch appears to defy gravity. In the real world, an arch with gaps in it can only fall, or rather, cannot even be erected.

---

[64]   *Phenomenology, Language and Society.   Selected Essays of Maurice Merleau-Ponty.* Ed. J. O'Neill (London, 1974), pp. 36-7

A third, and rather subtler model of how whole and parts relate can be glimpsed in Merleau-Ponty's use of the term *articulation* , though I do not think he is propounding this model. We could think of the parts as divisions and subdivisions of a previously undivided and undifferentiated totality, much as Saussure talks in terms of a language as the imposition of a form upon a substance. The image here is of a total field which the existing terms fill out by a process of spacing, to use a term adopted by Derrida. I shall consider this model further shortly. Suffice it to say for now that it is every bit as problematic as the other two, and makes no sense at all in relation to the acquisition of or changes in the sounds or the script of a language. There is no total field of sound to be divided up by the sounds in a language. Moreover, if by some chance we were all to be dropping our 'aitches' in a few years' time, there is absolutely nothing to compel us to compensate for this loss by adding extra aspiration to any or all of the surviving sounds in the language.

Since the differential view of language leads to such problems it is time to look critically at the positive arguments advanced in its favour. I shall consider first the Saussurean view of the *signifiant* as differentially determined, and then go on to consider the *signifié*.

One example Saussure gives of the differential interplay of linguistic elements is that of the individual characters in the written language. At least here we have a clearly delimited system insofar as there are a known finite number of identifiable characters within those languages using an alphabetic or phonetic script. Here Saussure cites the example of the letter 't' which in cursive script may take a variety of different forms. These variations are of no consequence argues Saussure, provided this letter is distinguishable differentially from others such as 'r' and 'l'. Unfortunately for his argument, this is simply not the case. A writer who adopted clearly defined yet idiosyncratic squiggles of his own however clearly distinguishable they might be from each other would be behaving in a way unacceptable to those trying to read his efforts. A 't' has to resemble the conventionally accepted forms of that letter rather than merely be distinct from all other letters. True, the history of writing could have been different, and a quite different set of written symbols could have been developed to convey the same information. But this does not make the writing system truly differential. Saussure claims that 'les valeurs de l'écriture n'agissent que par leur opposition réciproque au sein d'un sytème défini, composé d'un nombre déterminé de lettres', but the alleged reciprocity is spurious. Clearly if the letter 'a' is distinguishable from the letter 'b' then the letter 'b' is, by the same token, distinguishable from the letter 'a', but this is hardly a cogent argument against the view that letters of the alphabet do indeed have a positive identity. I cannot identify something as being the letter 'a' merely by demonstrating that that something is not one of the other twenty-five letters of the English alphabet. There is an infinity of things which are not letters of this alphabet at all which share this property, including, for example, all the letters of the Greek alphabet, the Taj Mahal, and a white Christmas, to name but a few.

In 1962 the BBC broadcast an elementary Russian course which introduced the Cyrillic alphabet by gradual stages to alleviate the task of mastering a strange script. Those following the course would have been surprised to learn that they were incapable of identifying the first few letters to which they had introduced until they knew what the rest of the alphabet was like. And many a school teacher will attest to the fact that a child can be taught to identify the letter 'a' before it has any inkling of the existence, let alone the form of the letter 'z'. Or to give one more example, if I am inventing my own shorthand system, I can make a start in designing the first few symbols before having completed in my mind a satisfactory total system. As I add to the repertoire of characters nothing has to happen to those already designed. They do not change their identity as the system expands.

If it were really true that we identified signifiers differentially then a cryptic text, produced by a simple substitution cypher, would be just as readable as the plain text on which it is based, because the same differential relationship between characters is to be found in both texts. But experience shows that it is not.

The same arguments apply to sound in spoken language, where indeed Saussure's own theory of the 'signifier' actually contradicts the differential theory. In discussing the signifier, Saussure notes that there will be slight variations in sound between individual utterances of the same word, but that these variations do not prevent correct identification. But surely, the fact that they do not is a clear indication that identification is not a purely differential process. Let us assume a simple phonetic system with only two sounds, a vowel 'v' which in practice occurs in different variants v_1, v_2, etc., and a consonant 'c' which in turn has variants c_1, c_2, etc. If users identified these sounds by a purely differential process, there would be nothing to enable them to conclude that v_2 was a variant of 'v' rather than of 'c' or indeed was not a phoneme in its own right. In fact, of course, recognition is possible because of perceived similarities between the actual sounds uttered and the repertoire of sounds which the listener expects to hear on the basis of past experience. This is positive identification. Variance implies deviation from a standard. And the existence of standards rules out the possibility of purely differential relationships amongst candidates for identification. We are dealing here with members of a class sharing some common property, or at least having what Wittgenstein termed a family resemblance. A purely differential phonetic system would rule out the possibility of there being any allophones, any variants of any particular phoneme.

If we turn now to semantic relationships, most of the arguments in favour of Saussure have concentrated on showing how different languages organise conceptual structures differently. The model adopted by the theorists is that of a total field being divided up in different ways by each language. The favourite example given is that of the colour terms in a language, which might be thought of as dividing up the spectrum. In effect, we are being invited to view the lexicon as a taxonomy. But for Saussure's differential theory to work, the taxonomy would have to be a perfect one, with no gaps and no overlapping between terms. But there do appear to be gaps in some languages which have very few colour terms. Indeed, there is no cultural reason why full coverage of the spectrum should be needed. Similarly, in a language like English, with a complex range of colour terms, there are obviously overlaps, turquoise, for example, overlapping blue and green. But even if we had a perfect system of colour terms, this would by no means demonstrate that individual colour terms have a differential rather than a positive identity. An apparent reference to positive standards is a common feature in many languages. What is there to say that the colour indigo does not owe its identity to the colour produced by the dye of that name rather than to its difference from the other colours of the rainbow. And who can prevent a child from learning the use of the adjective 'orange' by reference to the positive standard set by the fruit of that name rather than by a much more complicated differential process?

The unreality of the articulatory theory of the *signifié* emerges particularly strongly when one considers again the question of how anything can begin. For example, John Sturrock, in his introduction to *Structuralism and Since* , having said that each native language 'divides up in different ways the total field of what may be expressed in words', says:

> Without difference there can be no meaning. A one-term language is an impossibility because its single term could be applied to everything and differentiate nothing; it requires at least one other term to give it definition. It would be possible if rudimentary, to differentiate the entire contents of the universe by means of a two-term code or language, as being either *bing* or *bong*, perhaps. But without the introduction of that small phonetic difference, between the two vowel sounds, we can have no viable language at all.[65]

True, a single term *could* be applied to everything, but what would be the point? What Sturrock fails to say is that the linguistic equivalent of Parkinson's law, which says that *signifiés* expand to fill the conceptual space available actually *demands* that the less terms there are in a language, the more general they will have to be. So that a one-term language would theoretically be obliged to 'refer to everything.' Similarly, a two-term language would of necessity have to be a dichotomy.

A further complication in the argument is introduced by Jonathan Culler, when he says, in the same book:

> For a caveman successfully to originate language by making a special grunt signify something like 'food' is possible only if we assume that the grunt is already distinguished or distinguishable from other grunts and that the world has already been divided into the categories of food and non-food. Signification always depends on difference.[66]

---

65   *Structuralism and Since*, ed. John Sturrock (Oxford, Oxford University Press, 1979), p. 10

66   *Op.cit.*, 164

Does this mean that before the word 'everything' can enter a language the universe must be divided up into 'everything' and 'not-everything', and is 'not-everything' the same as 'nothing', 'something', 'anything' or none of these?

The simplest way to refute these views as to what is impossible in language is to invent a language in which the allegedly impossible comes true. The following is a description of one such language.

Imagine a tribe with a lexicon consisting of a single word comprising a single sound — /n/. Members of the tribe utter the word in order to dissuade. Typically the language is taught to children by a process of conditioning. An erring child is clipped round the ear or physically restrained at the same time the word is spoken. It eventually learns obedience when the sound alone is uttered. The tribe prospers as parents can keep their children out of danger while still having both hands free to carry goods, and, indeed, the simplicity of their phonetic system enables them to exercise their language while carrying things in their mouths.

The sole sound in the language is also capable of being used to different effect in different social circumstances. For example, it could be used playfully, accompanied by a smile, in mock rejection of an amorous advance. Or it could be used tauntingly by a group of chanting children mimicking a rather grumpy adult.

The only differential feature in the linguistic system I have described is that between the smile and the clip round the ear, differences not dreamed of in Saussure's philosophy.   But one does not have to experience or envisage all the social circumstances in which the word may be used in order to be said to know the language. The language has effectively been learned by the time a child responds to the Pavlovian conditioning inflicted on it by its parents.

Are we to say that the one sound in the language is differentially contrasted with silence? One problem here is that silence stands in the same relationship to any sound whatsoever, and not just this sound. Moreover, silence does not have one single value. There is a difference between vigilant silence, the silence of sleep, or the silent physical restraint of a child, which not only does not contrast with the uttering of 'n', but fulfils an identical function.

Let us assume that our imaginary language develops further. Presumably, if Saussurean theory is right, any new sound or new concept signified by it must necessarily stand in a contrasting reciprocal relationship to the one existing sound. No doubt the idea of a binary opposition of terms has a particular appeal to our increasingly computer conscious culture, but there is no practical or psychological reason why the language I have described should not develop in a quite different way.

Consider the following not implausible scenario. Thanks to a technological advance the tribe invent the shoulder bag, and lose the habit of carrying things in their mouths. Enjoying the new vocal freedom which this confers, some mothers add a vowel to the word 'n', and 'no' becomes standard, and functions alongside the existing 'n', the terms being totally interchangeable. The habit catches on of repeating the syllable 'no' in quickfire fashion, so that cries of 'nonono' become very common, to the extent that the linguistic theorist might decide that here we have a single three-syllable word rather than the repetition of a monosyllable.

All of this looks like bad news for the differential theory. Here we have a language which does originate with a single, positively identifiable term, and which develops by acquiring two more terms which fulfil an identical function, so that at each stage the alleged conceptual field remains intact at the level of the *signifié* whilst at the level of the *signifiant* we have a substantial overlap between 'n', 'no' and 'nonono', and there is no way at any stage to see what happens here as the articulation of a total field.

The fact that my example is an imaginary one is of no consequence, since there is nothing to prevent it becoming fact. We could teach it to our babies as a first language without difficulty.

Before we are too harsh on Saussure for the inadequacy of the differential theory, we should bear in mind that his teachings come down to us in the form of a reconstruction made from his pupils' notes. He acknowledged the difficulty of saying anything sensible about language, and was clearly not satisfied that his lecture courses were publishable as they stood , and apparently retained no notes of them himself. Moreover, his bold initial statements about the role of difference are later qualified quite dramatically. The post-structuralists seem to have overlooked the following passage, which borders on a recantation of the theory he has just expounded.

> Mais dire que tout est négatif dans la langue, cela n'est vrai que du signifié et du signifiant pris séparément. Dès que l'on considère le signe dans sa totalité, on se trouve en présence d'une chose positif dans son ordre... Deux signes comportant chacun un signifié et un signifiant ne sont pas différents, ils sont seulement distincts. Entre eux il n'y a qu'*opposition*. Tout le mécanisme du langage... repose sur des oppositions de ce genre et sur les différences phoniques et conceptuelles qu'elles impliquent.[67]

So here we have the rather bizarre situation that the constituent parts of the sign are differentially determined, but the sign is not. What we are to make of this distinction without a difference is hard to fathom. Suffice it to say that semiotics is such an insecure discipline and the sign so elusive that there is no possible means of ascertaining how many signs there are in a sentence such as this one.

It seems then, that there is no credible account of how a language could have difference as its essential basis. As we have seen, Derrida is aware of at least some of the objections to the differential theory, and it is interesting to see the role he gives to what he terms *la différance* as a response to some of these difficulties.

Seen in traditional terms, Derrida's strategy here, as indeed elsewhere in the theory of deconstruction, is to give us the *reductio ad absurdum* of a point of view. But then

---

67   *Op.cit.*, 166-7

instead of accepting the logical consequences and regarding the resulting impossibility as grounds for rejecting the theory which has given rise to it, he almost seems to regard the theory as reinforced by the absurdity. *La différance*, which of necessity he can only speak of in the most mysterious terms, is in effect a device introduced to 'explain' the impossible. For him it is, amongst other things, 'the production of a system of differences'. But from a rational point of view there can be no such thing as a system of differences. As we have seen, difference is not capable of determining the function of elements in a system which involves a degree of redundancy and overlap, or choices between functionally equivalent alternatives. Nor can difference be used as a helpful criterion in a system whose precise limits are not known, because elements in a system differ not only from each other but also from other elements which are outside the system altogether. But language as a whole, and individual languages in particular, have no precise limits, are infinitely adaptable, and have many elements of which individual users are ignorant. No user of a language, for example, will have a vocabulary which approaches the size of that given in any of the major dictionaries. It follows that in practice nobody can be using difference as the primary factor in getting to grips with a language.

The above excursion into the theory of Saussure and his followers shows that it provides no grounds for doubting the validity of the distinction between literal and figurative language. Ultimately the argument in favour of seeing language as having a literal base is that without regularities a language would be unlearnable, and therefore useless. Consider the offspring of a couple of jocular parents who habitually used the trope of irony, referring to hot things as cold and cold things as hot. Let us assume that they do this in a dead-pan way without offering any clues to their ironic intentions in their tone of voice or facial expression. If they were consistently ironic all the time, then the child would pick up their habits, and, having no other basis to go on, would almost certainly treat 'cold' as literally meaning 'hot' and vice-versa. It would be right to do so, in that the trope would have become lexicalized as a standard part of the parents' language. On making contact with a wider society, the child might then assume that others were being ironic in their use of the two terms. As its experience widened it might then recognize its own parents as being out of step. But if its parents used 'cold' to mean 'hot' exactly half of the time and to mean 'cold' the other half, the result would be a word with no useful function and whose meaning could not be learned. Without a literal base language can have no use.

Having laid out the basis for distinguishing the literal from the figurative, it remains for me to justify briefly my considering trope as a phenomenon operating at the level of individual words, a view which is challenged by Paul Ricoeur in his remarkable book on metaphor.[68] Ricoeur sees semantics as opposed to semiotics, as

---

68   Paul Ricoeur, *The Rule of Metaphor*, translated by R. Czerny (London, Routledge & Kegan Paul, 1978)

having its basis in the sentence as a grammatical unit, and argues that metaphor is a kind of predication. True, it is only through its context that we recognize a trope as such. But this does not make the context itself a trope. A sentence may, and in Góngora's case frequently does, contain a multiplicity of separately identifiable tropes. Moreover, to take the sentence as a unit is too limiting. Contextual clues not only overflow the limits of the sentence at times, but may be pragmatic rather than dependent on other words in a text. For example, in order to recognize the irony of the greeting "Good evening" addressed to a late riser at the breakfast table, the relevant context is the time of day, not anything else which may or may not have been said. Again, to see metaphor as essentially a question of predication is too limiting. Firstly, tropes do not confine themselves to what is grammatically the predicate of a sentence. The subject of a sentence is just as likely a candidate. Secondly, tropes may be found just as readily in questions, which assert nothing, as in the rather better behaved predicatory sentences which Ricoeur seems to have in mind.

To summarise our findings in this chapter, then, literal language, from which trope is a deviation, is effectively the set of semantic regularities in the use of words or expressions perceived by learners of a language without which the language would be both useless and unlearnable. These regularities are neither prescriptive nor unchanging, but shift according to the changing habits of the users of a language. The habitual use of particular expressions in a way which was initially perceived as deviant, for example, may lead to their acceptance as standard and part of the literal base. How they are perceived ultimately depends on the experience of individuals. A regular reader of Góngora is likely to react in a different way to his most common metaphors than one for whom his poetry is a new experience.

Chapter Four: The varieties of trope

When it comes to considering the contribution of figurative language to the sharpness of Góngora's wit, a tendency to concentrate exclusively on metaphor, the trope of resemblance, has perhaps prevented a full appreciation of his complexity, subtlety and the sheer variety of his inventive genius. As we shall see, not only does Góngora use the full repertoire of recognised classical tropes, but combines them in interesting ways, and even produces what seem to be new kinds of trope as yet unclassified.

The various kinds of trope are classifiable according to the type of linguistic manœuvre which is required in order to obtain a reading which makes sense. Their categorization depends on the precise way in which they deviate from literal usage. A useful tool for analysis is the study of the logical relationship between what a trope refers to literally, and nonsensically, and what it must refer to figuratively if the nonsense is to be dispelled. In the case of metaphor, the relationship between the literal referent, and what I shall call the effective referent is one of resemblance. Of the remaining tropes recognized in classical rhetoric, those of hyperbole and litotes, alias overstatement and understatement, involve a difference of degree between the literal and effective referents, requiring the reader to strengthen or weaken the literal force of the trope. With irony, the relationship is one of opposition, where what is to be understood is the opposite of what is literally said. In the case of synecdoche, the individual relationships specified in the manuals of rhetoric, those between genus and species, singular and plural, part and whole, and between the material from which an object is made and the object itself can justifiably be linked together as involving what could be called a participatory relationship, such as the relationship between a member and the class to which it belongs, or between a class and a sub-class. Examples of metonymy given in traditional theory, however, are more difficult to fit into a general pattern. They include the relationship between cause and effect, possessor and possession, creator and artefact, container and contents. In general, the relationship is one of association, and the question is whether there is any general principle at work here, or whether metonymy should be seen as a kind of rag-bag which includes any trope based upon a relationship of association which is not classifiable as synecdochic.

Paul Ricoeur contrasts metonymy and synecdoche as involving co-ordination and subordination respectively.[69] Yet there is more than a hint of hierarchy or subordination in the types of metonymic relationships mentioned above. My own explanation is that the relationship between the first and second terms in each pair

---

[69]   *The Rule of Metaphor, Op.cit.*, 119.

(cause/effect, container/contained) is one of control, with the first controlling the second. Hence, the owner controls his possessions, the container controls its contents, the cause controls the effect. Such a relationship is distinguishable from the participatory one involved in synecdoche.

The range of tropes outlined above have not received equal critical attention. In particular metaphor has tended to hog the limelight. However, a revival of interest in rhetoric among French theorists in particular has partly reversed a process of decline which is summarized by Ricoeur in these terms

> Since the Greeks, rhetoric diminished bit by bit to a theory of *style* by cutting itself off from the two parts that generated it, the theories of *argumentation* and of *composition*. Then, in turn, the theory of style shrank to a classification of figures of speech, and this to a theory of tropes. Tropology itself now paid attention only to the complex made up of metaphor and metonymy, at the price of reducing the first to resemblance and the second to contiguity.[70]

This has resulted in the rescue of synecdoche, which analysis shows is not reducible to metonymy as Jakobson had claimed.[71] Yet it still remains true that scant attention has been paid to hyperbole, and its converse litotes, which if one is looking for general principles to which all tropes could be reduced provide a credible model. Metaphor can be regarded as a kind of overstatement because it equates things which are not identical but merely similar. Synecdoche where the part represents the whole, or the singular represents the plural and vice versa can also be seen as a form of understatement or overstatement. The same could probably be said of metonyms where interchanges between the controller and the controlled could be seen in the same terms.

Generally speaking, the attempt to reduce all tropes to a single formula, interesting though the challenge may be, is unhelpful in the practical analysis of complex examples, where greater clarity can be achieved by considering the full range of logical relationships. But the ability of hyperbole to overlap with other tropes helps to make it one of the most elusive types of figurative language. Moreover, as we shall see in the following chapter, its chameleon-like quality is such that we are sometimes left in doubt whether to interpret it as a trope at all.

If we were trying to reverse the reductive approach to the theory of trope and question whether the classical canon of types of trope is broad enough to include all possibilities, one starting point might be to check them against Cicero's list of Topics or alternatively Aristotle's categories which the theorists of wit saw as a comprehensive tool for specifying the logical relationships underlying the conceit. It is interesting to see how these relationships relate to those involved in the traditional repertoire of tropes.

---

70   *Op.cit.*, 45
71   See, e.g., R. Jakobson, 'Two aspects of language and two types of aphasic disfunction', in his *Language in Literature*, (Harvard, 1987), Chapter Eight.

The topics of the whole and the parts, and of genus and species correspond to synecdoche, cause and effect to metonymy, similarity (and possibly dissimilarity) to metaphor, the comparison of greater and lesser to hyperbole and litotes, and contraries to irony. This leaves the linguistically based topics 'conjugates' (words of different grammatical form derived from the same roots) and 'etymology', which provide headings which could account for some puns, but it is hard to see how tropes as such could be based on them. We also have to account for three remaining Topics, 'adjuncts' 'antecedents' and 'consequents'. Antecedents and consequents involve a relationship between events following each other which falls short of a cause/effect link. Such a relationship could provide the basis for a trope, and would no doubt be perceived as a kind of metonymy rather than a fundamentally new trope. The relationship between lightning and thunder might be a case in point. As for the Topic of 'adjuncts', which means 'corollaries', that is, things readily inferred from others, the problem in using this as a basis for a trope is that the inferences we make are whole propositions. They are statements about things as opposed to mere things as in the case of causes and effects, etc.

These considerations might suggest that the classical repertoire of tropes exhausts the repertoire of usable logical relationships. But Góngora, as always, has a few tricks up his sleeve, and, as we shall see shortly, some of his techniques refuse to fit comfortably into any hitherto recognized scheme. His poetry encourages us to expand our theoretical horizons rather than accept the limited diet of mere metaphor with which many critics seem to be content.

The relative lack of interest in tropes other than metaphor amongst theorists is no doubt partly the result of an assumption that metaphor is the trope which requires the greatest flexibility of interpretation because the relationship of resemblance, on which it is based, seems somehow more complicated than that between part and whole, or between singular and plural on which synecdoches may be based. One flaw in this assumption is that tropes do not come ready labelled in a text according to their various types. We do not know in advance what species of trope we may be dealing with when a text deviates from literal language. If we were in the habit of assuming any trope we came across was a metaphor, then when we encountered a synecdoche we would actually be engaged in a more complicated interpretative process. In principle, no one type of trope is any more or less complicated than any other. In practice, Góngora's poetry demonstrates both the power and the subtlety of some of the underprivileged tropes.

If there is a tendency to think of the so-called metaphor *in praesentia*, where the two terms of the comparison are both named, as a relatively unexciting trope because it gives the game away, one might have expected a metonymy *in praesentia* to be plain dull. But Góngora's phrase explaining that the shepherd in his poem 'Donde las altas ruedas' (Millé 387) chose to sit under an ash tree 'porque su sombra es flores' belies this assumption. 'Flores' here is not a metaphor because there is no resemblance between shade and flowers, but it does make sense when read as a metonymy where the contents, the flowers, stand in for what contains them, the shade, both terms in the relationship being named. The result is nonetheless poetically interesting.

The use of synecdoche to dramatic effect can be seen in stanza 22 of his *Polifemo*.

> Mudo la noche el can, el día dormido
> de cerro en cerro y sombra en sombra yace.
> Bala el ganado. Al mísero balido
> nocturno el lobo de las sombras nace. (lines 169-172)

Here the inactivity of the island's dogs as they stretch out on the hilltops and sleep in the shadows is described using only singular nouns set in a framework of pleasing symmetry. Góngora matches the singular form of the synecdoche 'el can', which is placed in a line which grammatically speaking is palindromic in form, with the singular nouns in the following line through the use of 'de... en...' structure. It is also worth noting the symmetrical correspondence of each half line with that of its neighbouring line. During the heat of midday the dogs sleep in the shade, at night they recline on the hilltops (most unlikely to provide protection during the day, but cooler than the plains at night). The effect of the synecdoche is to enhance the dramatic vividness of the passage by encouraging us to visualize a particular scene — one which is repeated all over the island. We can follow the symmetrical pattern further by reading 'el lobo' as again synecdochic. We can assume there is more than one wolf, but the emotional impact is enhanced by a trope which encourages us to envisage one particular villain.

Metonymy is another trope which is capable of a poetic effect every bit as powerful as any metaphor. A notable example is Góngora's description of the shipwrecked young man struggling up the cliff at dusk, blundering through the thorny undergrowth, as 'entre espinas crepúsculos pisando'. If we ask ourselves what the young man is literally walking on, then logically it must be the ground or whatever is lying on it. The use of the plural of 'crepúsculo', a noun not normally admitting a plural, invites us to think of things on the ground rather than the ground itself, things which are all contained within the dusk, and rendered indistinct by the controlling gloom.

It is interesting to note here that the unconventional use of the plural does not imply that 'crepúsculos' is doing duty as a replacement for some other specific plural noun which would supply the literal meaning. The very power of this metonymy derives from our inability to identify precisely what the poet might be referring to. Góngora's viewpoint is not that of the omniscient narrator, but that of the young man who in the increasing darkness is unable to see clearly what he is treading on, an unsettling situation which could lead one to imagine all kinds of horrors.

A similar example can be found near the start of *Las firmezas de Isabela*, where Marcelo talks of the insecurity afflicting the lover

> Si tinieblas no pisa con pie incierto
> entre escollos y arenas

con leño frágil solicita el puerto. (lines 10-12)

Here the situation is complicated by the fact that the physical elements are symbolic, so that the metonymy 'tinieblas' is at the same time a metaphor set within a sequence of metaphors which function together in allegorical fashion.

There is a closely parallel use of this type of metonymy in Quevedo's *Sermón estoico de censura moral*, when he envisages greedy men desecrating graves as they dig for subterranean treasures 'palpando miedos'.[72] Again we have the unusual plural of 'miedo', the metonymy here being based on the cause/effect relationship. The groping hands touch things which cause horror. The fact that these things are unnamed heightens the emotional effect. We are dealing with the unspeakable, maybe with things too horrible to imagine. Like the dreaded Room 101 in Huxley's *Nineteen Eighty-Four* the horror is heightened by being left to the individual's own imagination.

It is doubtful whether all the above examples of synecdoche and metonymy can be regarded as examples of wit, though on the grounds of its beautiful symmetry the passage from the *Polifemo* might as a whole elicit admiration for its *correspondencias*. The metonymies expressing insecurity achieve their effect in the opposite way from conceits which rely on the shock of recognition. However this does not mean that the seemingly simple trope of synecdoche, for example, cannot provide striking conceits, particularly when used in combination.

Some of Góngora's seventeenth century critics complained about his use of compound metaphor. For example, Francisco Cascales saw the obcurity of Góngora's *Polifemo* as caused partly by 'metáforas tan contínuas, que se descubren unas a otras, y aun a veces están unas sobre otras.'[73] Góngora was also said to have metaphorized metaphor. But in principle a metaphor of a metaphor is an unworkable trope. If object A can be referred to by a term which normally designates a similar object B, and object B can be represented in turn by a term literally referring to a similar object C it does not follow that the term for C is likely to prove a comprehensible metaphor for object A. If objects A and C have no obvious common features then the attempt at a metaphor will be too enigmatic in the absence of any pointer to the intermediary object B. On the other hand if there is an obvious overlap between A and C then consideration of B becomes redundant. The problem is that both tropes rely on the same relationship, resemblance. However, compound tropes involving different kinds of relationship are a more practical proposition.

Consider the trope, already commonplace in classical times, where 'tree' means 'ship'. In its standard use in Latin it is already a compound trope, and a further layer of trope is arguably added when a specific type of tree is chosen. Pine, beech and oak are all variants found in Góngora, but if the reader is not much concerned with the

---

[72]   *Obras completas*, Vol 1, *Poesía original*, ed. J.M. Blecua, (Barcelona, Planeta, 1968), p.130, poem 145, line 20.

[73]   *Cartas filológicas*, I,8. I quote from A. Martínez Arancón, *La batalla en torno a Góngora* (Barcelona, Bosch, 1978), p. 198.

particular species of tree then we have a synecdoche in which the species of tree represents the genus. In turn the tree represents what the boat is made from, another kind of synecdoche. Finally the part/whole relationship is also involved since part of the tree is used to make perhaps only part of the boat. An alternative analysis would take us through a different route of multiple synecdoches with the tree representing the tree trunk, the trunk representing a coracle made from a hollowed out trunk, and the genus coracle in turn representing the species boat. A third route of analysis suggests itself, though the specific instances of tropes referring to boats in Góngora tend not to support it as a correct one, is that 'pine' represents the pinewood from which the pine tree is made, and that in turn represents the boat made from the wood. Behind this well-worn trope, which is so moribund if not dead as to attract little attention, we have a complex double or triple synecdoche. Góngora's wit adds further strands of trope to the image and revives it. For example, the sonnet beginning

velero bosque de árboles poblado

que visten hojas de inquieto lino (Millé 283)

adds a metaphorical strand to the image by observing the similarity with a tree with its leaves and a mast with its sails. The collective noun 'bosque' adds yet another twist, which again insofar as it is based on an analogy is metaphorical. As a fleet is to a ship, so is a wood to a tree. His earlier ode on the Spanish armada which suppresses any explicit reference to trees places extra demands on the reader

Tú, que con celo pío y noble saña

el seno undoso al húmido Neptuno

de selvas inquietas has poblado... (Millé 385)

following the lexicalised dead metaphor 'seno' and the similarly conventional metonymy Neptune=sea, Góngora presents the reader with his mobile forests, which as well as being built on an analogy developed from the conventional multiple synecdoche of the tree can also be seen as having a further metaphorical dimension in that a group of ships with their many masts could be seen as physically resembling a forest. The past participle 'poblado' can be seen as a further metaphor, though the fact that there are crews of men on board the vessels might lead us to read 'poblado' literally and to further enrich our reading of the word 'selvas' to include not just the boats but the men on them — a further strand of synecdoche, with the part standing for the whole.

The clustering together, as in this last example, of mutually interacting tropes which themselves may be compound can lead to some remarkable conceits. An example involving synecdoche again is found in the dedication to Góngora's *Soledades* where he invites the Duke of Béjar to rest from his hunting activities:

arrima a un frexno el frexno cuyo acero

en tiempo hará breve

purpurear la nieve. (lines 13-15)

Here we can identify 'el frexno cuyo acero...' as the Duke's spear where 'ash' refers to the ash wood from which its shaft is made. The following synecdoche 'acero' identifying the steel blade at its tip modifies our interpretation of 'el frexno' which we might otherwise be tempted to identify as a staff rather than a spear. Thus we have a multiple synecdoche where 'frexno' represents the wood from the tree, which in turn represents the shaft from which it is made, which in turn represents the whole spear of which the shaft is a part. Much of the sharpness of this conceit derives from a relationship not of similarity but in this case of identity. There is a peculiar aptness in the Duke being invited to rest his spear against the same kind of tree from which it was fashioned. There is the possibility that by some quirk of fate the Duke could even select the same tree from which it was taken, and his action could represent a kind of temporary restoration of the branch to the tree from which it was originally taken.

As far as conceits based on metaphor are concerned, in general the more points of resemblance established between the real and the effective referents the more apt the *correspondencia* is likely to seem. In the case of Góngora's description near the start of his *Soledades,* of the ocean to which the young seafarer commits his life as 'una Libia de ondas' (I, 20), a compound trope consisting of synecdoche plus metaphor, where 'Libia' represents the genus 'desert', the comparison between desert and ocean can readily developed as we compare their vastness, inhospitability, and detailed correspondences between waves and dunes, tempests and sandstorms, and note at the same time the obvious contrast between the wet and the dry. But no specific guidance is given by Góngora here as to how far to pursue the parallel. To display wit more overtly the poet needs to take his reader specifically through some of the more unexpected possibities underlying a metaphor. Illustrations of how this can be achieved are seen in Góngora's witty development of the commonplace metaphor of referring to a spring as a snake on the basis of the similarity of shape in the second *Soledad.*

> Ella pues sierpe, y sierpe al fin pisada,
> aljófar vomitando fugitivo
> en lugar de veneno,
> torcida esconde, ya que no enroscada,
> las flores, que de un parto dió lascivo
> aura fecunda al matizado seno
> del huerto, en cuyos troncos se desata
> de las escamas que vistió de plata. (II, 320-27)

The water thrown into the air as the spring strikes the trunk of a tree is envisaged as a spitting of poision by the snake which has been trodden on by the foot of a tree. Twisting, but not coiled, the 'snake' pursues its course, shedding some of its silvery scales (foam, no doubt) on the tree trunks.

In the first *Soledad* the gloomy old man's refusal to imitate the young girls who are splashing about in and drinking from the waters of the spring is ingeniously interpreted as a fear of being poisoned by the snakes.

> ... a cuantos da la fuente

sierpes de aljófar aun mayor veneno

que a las de el Ponto, tímido, atribuye,

según el pie, según los labios huye. (lines 598-601)

Sometimes where Góngora provides a sequence of interacting tropes the rhetorical complexity of a passage defies analysis. The following two lines offer an instructive example.

Músicas hojas viste el menor ramo

del álamo que peina verdes canas (lines 590-91)

Many of the words in this passage are capable of being interpreted as figurative. Although Góngora begins by referring literally to the smallest branch of the tree, presumably this is a synecdochic reference to every branch of the tree. There is a kind of tacit *a fortiori* argument here. If even a twig is covered in leaves then how leafy the whole tree must be. 'Viste', which in isolation would be a dead metaphor, is revitalised by the use of 'peina' in the following line, which in turn encourages us to see the tree as personified, dressing and combing itself. As for the musical leaves, the most obvious interpretation leads us to assume that Góngora is referring to the rustling of the leaves in the breeze, understanding 'hojas' literally and 'músicas' as possibly metonymic, with 'musical' meaning 'pleasant sounding', the species representing the genus. But the reference in the following line to breezes and nightingales being in the tree suggests another ingenious interpretation which by no means excludes the obvious one. The birds themselves could be musical leaves, in which case 'hojas' is read as a metaphor, and 'músicas' is understood literally.[74]

However, a third magical possibility suggests itself, which is that the observer hearing the rustling leaves and the song of the birds but not seeing the birds hidden amongst the dense foliage might innocently think that the leaves of the tree are singing, in which case we would take 'músicas hojas' to be a literal expression rather than a trope. Its literal status in no way diminishes its wit, with the poet's feigned innocence offering an ingenious account of events from the point of view of one taken in by deceptive appearances.

The phrase 'peina verdes canas' provides the final challenge. The metaphor 'peina' suggests the way the breeze moves the leaves, but the contradictory 'verdes canas' is easier to understand than it is to classify rhetorically. Insofar as it means 'hair', 'canas' functions as a straightforward metaphor, but its implicit adjectival aspect, for 'canas' are white hairs, clashes with the preceding adjective 'verdes'. One way of resolving the clash would be to read 'canas' as a metonymic reference to the venerable age of the tree — its leaves are green, but it is of an age one associates with white hair. Another would be to see its leaves as being greenish white in colour, in which case we might read 'verde' as hyperbolic, or understand that we are in effect dealing with an implicit compound adjective green-white. One can see a similar technique

---

[74] In another poem Góngora refers to nightingales as the fruit of a tree 'porque su sombra es flores/su dulce fruto dulces ruiseñores' (Millé 387).

used by Góngora to describe the mixture of red and white wines in the peasants' glasses as 'topacios carmesíes/y pálidos rubíes' (I 870), where the adjectives can be seen as hyperbolic modifiers of the metaphorical nouns.   But another poem of Góngora's suggests that he has a quite different interpretation in mind. The aspen is a tree whose leaves are green on one side, and a silvery white on the other. Góngora's *romancillo* 'Frescos airecillos' (Millé 29) acknowledges this when he describes

> álamos crecidos
> de hojas inciertas
> medias de esmeraldas
> y de plata medias.

Perhaps we could analyse 'canas' as a metaphor plus a synecdoche, in which the whole leaf represents a part, the white half of the leaf, whilst the adjective 'verdes' in complementary fashion should be seen as synecdochic applying only to part of the leaf — the other half. This is conceptually quite difficult to take on board, and not wholly convincing as an explanation of what is happening rhetorically.   Comparison with another passage in which Góngora paradoxically mixes green and white is instructive and suggests yet another approach.

At the start of his second *Soledades* Góngora describes the turbulent meeting point between a stream and the sea, referring to

> el padre de las aguas
> coronado de blancas ovas y espuma verde. (lines 24-5)

Here the weed which one would have expected to be green is described as white, and in complementary fashion foam which is normally white is described as green. It seems unlikely that we are supposed to take these expressions at face value. Surely the weed cannot literally be white, though the foam on it may hide its true colour. Similarly the foam is not itself white, though the weed within it may modify our perception. In effect Góngora has mirrored a perceptually confusing scene in which there is a turbulent intermingling of weed and foam with a corresponding confusion at the linguistic level.   The use of counterbalanced phrases sets the tropes within a figure with adds further clarity, but this is clearly not a case of a hyperbaton for 'verdes ovas y espuma blanca'. The final 'espuma verde' could be deleted without any loss of logic, though the result would lack the agreeable symmetry of the passage as it stands. What we seem to have here is a complex trope in which noun and adjective function together, pulling in opposite directions. The paradoxical phrase points to an illusion or simply a confusion of the senses which admits of a rational explanation. The relationship between what is literally referred to and what effectively we are to understand is the relation between the illusory, logically impossible appearance, and the reality which we know intellectually must underly it.   This trope of illusion seems to have been a personal invention of Góngora's.

One further illustration of the same technique, again in the field of colour, is Góngora's famous description of Galatea's complexion in his *Polifemo*

Duda el amor cual más su color sea

o púrpura nevada o nieve roja. (lines 107-8)

Galatea's admiring beholders ('el amor' is perhaps a metonymic reference to those who love her rather than Cupid) are overwhelmed at the sight of her magnificent colouring, attracted now to her red cheeks, now to the no less stunning whiteness of the surrounding skin. Unable to settle on either with both vying so strongly for attention the lover is reduced to a confusion which is reflected in the counterbalanced paradoxical phrases 'púrpura nevada' and 'nieve roja'.

In the series of paradoxical images of colour we have just looked at and that of the singing tree the relationship between the literal and effective referents is that between how things might appear to the naive observer, and how they look to somebody more experienced. In one sense the relationship between appearance and reality might seem to fit the trope of metaphor. But there is an important ingredient limiting and defining the relationship more closely and distinguishing it from metaphor, namely, the deception of the senses. In the case of Góngora's musical leaves, neither the music nor the leaves are metaphors for something else. What is described is not there because it resembles something else which is not described. Both music and leaves are physically present at the scene. It is the unconventional way in which they are related which constitutes the special quality of this trope of illusion, if trope it be.[75]

In the light of these examples if we look afresh at one of Góngora's most famous images from near the start of the first *Soledad* we shall see that what has traditionally been described by the critics as a metaphor turns out to be nothing of the sort. With a storm at sea, in the fading light the horizon offers a confused mix of waves and mountains:

No bien, pues, de su luz los horizontes

que hacían montes de agua y piélagos de montes,

desdorados los siente ... (lines 42-5)

If we read the phrase 'montes de agua' as a metaphor for a stormy sea and 'piélagos de montes' as a metaphor for a mountain range in which the hills are shaped like waves the result makes little logical sense. It is not that the horizon made waves and mountain ranges, but that it made mountains out of waves and waves out of mountains. If we then try to 'translate' the phrases as metaphors we end up with nothing meaningful: the horizon making waves out of waves and mountains out of mountains. The image does work, however, if we see this as an example of the trope of illusion. Both mountains and waves are literally present, but hard to distinguish in the prevailing conditions and are easily confused by the observer. Another way of looking at this passage is to regard the verb 'hacer' as a trope for 'hacer parecer'.

---

[75] Tesauro recognized the special appeal of optical illusion as the basis for conceits, referring to it as the 'mirabile per opinione'.

Another fascinating instance of Góngora juggling with elements which are all literally present in a scene is to be found in his description of the pastoral setting in his *Romance de Angélica y Medoro* (Millé 48). But on this occasion we are not dealing with the deception of the senses. Near the start of the poem he describes the rustic retreat:

> Do la paz viste pellico
> y conduce entre pastores
> ovejas del monte al llano
> y cabras del llano al monte. (lines 5-6)

Sharply observing the opposite directions in which the sheep and the goats go to their pastures, a conceit which one could imagine amusingly expressed through the alternative medium of an animated cartoon, Góngora makes 'paz' the subject of the verb 'conduce'.

The idea of peace being dressed in a sheepskin coat invites two relatively straightforward metonymic interpretations. We can either see the sheep themselves, who slightly ironically, in a way which is half literal and half figurative can be thought of as wearing sheepskin coats, or we can regard the shepherds that guide them as symbolizing peace. This would give us a metonym based on the relationship between possessor and possessed, those who enjoy peace, and the peace they enjoy. But when we reach the second line 'y conduce entre pastores' there is a kind of mismatch which prevents either of these two versions working totally happily. If peace is providing the guidance and it is the sheep that are being guided, then the sheep themselves cannot be the literal subject of the verb behind 'la paz' read as a metonym. On the other hand, if it is the shepherds that epitomize peace, what are we to make of the ironic redundancy of these same shepherds in the second line? We might be tempted to interpret the passage iconically and paint ourselves a mental picture of a figure clad in a shepherd's coat engaged in shepherding activities. But for this to be worthwhile there would have to be some significance behind such a picture. We still have to search for the figurative significance behind the literal representation. Góngora stresses the peacefulness of rural activities by expressing himself in such a way as to make peace the controlling factor, the active subject of the verb. Although in literal terms it must be the shepherds which are guiding the flocks, this prosaic role is diminished in importance by the structure which Góngora uses. If we look at what is happening from a grammatical standpoint, instead of giving us the expected structure with shepherds as the subject guiding their sheep 'in peace', using such an adverbial phrase to qualify the verb, Góngora in effect converts the adverbial phrase into the subject of the sentence and vice versa, with peace guiding the sheep amid shepherds. The technique offers a powerful source of hyperbole which is easily enough adapted to other contexts, but again it is one in which the different elements in the sentence mutually interact in a way which the classical theory of trope is ill equipped to cope with.

Not only does Góngora use the whole range of traditionally recognized tropes, then, often combining them in complex clusters, but he also takes the would-be theorist into uncharted territory. As for the conventionally recognized tropes, I have argued that hyperbole, which figures prominently in Gracián's *agudeza de ponderación*, deserves a more central theoretical place than it has normally been granted. In practical terms, hyperbole is one of the most difficult tropes to analyze. This is not only because, as has been indicated in this chapter, it overlaps with other tropes, but also because it sometimes seems to inhabit an terrain which is neither wholly figurative nor wholly literal. The way Góngora exploits the interplay between trope and literal language is the topic of my next chapter.

Chapter Five: Between the literal and the figurative

The semantic patterns produced by the literal reading of tropes in their context can make an important contribution to our perception of how sharp the wit is in a particular passage. Except in the rare cases where literal and figurative readings both work perfectly, all tropes involve a kind of mismatch at the literal level, and it is precisely this which helps us to identify them as tropes in the first place. If we are consideringSarbiewski's definition of wit as a 'discordia concors' we might be tempted to identify the discord with this mismatch. But this would fail to distinguish between routine tropes and those which display wit. For a more fruitful analysis we need to distinguish between different ways of not making sense at the literal level.

Sometimes the literal reading of trope results in contradictions which are identifiable as oxymoron or to a pattern of opposition closely resembling this figure. In such cases the sense of discord within harmony is sharp, and Tesauro gives the name 'il mirabile', the marvellous, to such figures, seeing them as a particularly powerful source of wit. In fact he casts the net a little more widely in defining 'il mirabile' as taking one of three possible enigmatic forms of which the combination between positive and negative is one, the others consisting of positive plus positive and negative plus negative.

Tesauro illustrates the various forms of this figure by giving a series of descriptions of an echo repeating one's voice. Thus, combining positive and negative we could say of the echo:

> Ella e un'anima inanime, mutola insieme e faconda, che parla senza lingua; uomo e non uomo.[76]

What happens here is that a literal reading produces a contradiction which resolves itself once we read the tropes as tropes. Hence 'parla', which incidentally personifies the echo, is a trope which identifies the passive reproduction of vocal sound with the active controlled use of vocal equipment. The mere reflection of sound does not require a tongue, and the contradiction emerges only when we read the phrase literally.

The combination of positive and positive is illustrated thus by Tesauro:

> Ella e ninfa dell'aria, pietra parlante, scoglio animato, figlia del fiato; abita nelle selve e parla tutti gli idiomi

---

[76]   *Trattatisti e narratori del seicento, Op.cit.,*91

Here the combinations of qualities are puzzling or unusual without being strictly speaking contradictory. Standard nymphs do not float in the air. Normal rocks do not speak.

Once again the trick involves trope. The nymph is not really a nymph. The rock does not really speak. Interestingly enough this particular trope of the speaking rock could be seen as an example of the trope of illusion we identified as an original creation of Góngora's. To the innocent observer the echoing rock might give the illusion of speaking.

Finally, combining negative with negative, we might say:

Non e uomo e non e fiera. Non sa parlare né tacere...

The puzzling feature here is that within each pair of statements the possibilities seem to have been exhausted when we read the phrases literally, leaving us by a process of elimination with an impossibility.

Góngora frequently exploits the disconcerting patterns of Tesauro's 'mirabile' which emerge when we read tropes literally. One of his earliest poems, a light-hearted poem in which the poet protests at being importuned by Cupid begins with several examples:

Ciego que apuntas, y atinas
caduco dios, y rapaz,
vendado que me has vendido,
y niño mayor de edad,
por el alma de tu madre,
--que murió siendo inmortal,
de invidia de mi señora--
que no me persigas más. (Millé 1)

The paradox in the opening line of the blind archer unerringly hitting the target is perhaps not so much a case of a literal reading of 'ciego' and 'atinas' as tropes as a sharp juxtaposition of qualities traditionally ascribed to a mythical god which seem on the face of it to be incompatible. This is not to say that the ideas of love being blind and of love striking home do not make sense in metaphorical terms. But Góngora has constructed his poem as an address to a personalised god. The second line mixes opposites of age. The god is both senile ('caduco') and young ('rapaz'), both a child and an adult ('niño mayor de edad'). These thoughts could prompt a critical reflection on the status of a mythical being like Cupid, who is not only immortal but apparently never grows up. We can see the adjectives referring to old age as tropes here. It is the myth of Cupid being a child that is centuries old.

Passing over the play on words contrasting Cupid as 'vendado' and the poet as 'vendido', we arrive at the description of Venus dying, despite being immortal. Góngora keeps us waiting here for the phrase 'de envidia de mi señora' so that we have already sensed the opposition between immortality and death before we realize that what we have on our hands is a dead metaphor rather than a dead goddess.

Negative and positive can be seen in potent combination in the mature Góngora in his description of the awed response to the magnificent view from a hilltop in the first *Soledad*.:

> Muda la admiración habla callando ·
> y ciega, un río sigue... (lines 197-8)

The dumbstruck viewer reveals his wonder by his silence. Góngora not only gives us the literal contradiction between the verbs 'hablar and 'callar', but heightens the expression of wonderment by personifying wonder using the metonymic 'la admiración' to refer to the amazed onlooker. The verb 'sigue', here obviously means 'follow with the eye', and clashes with the adjectival trope 'ciega'.

The majority of examples of 'il mirabile' in Góngora consist in the combination of positive with positive. In other words they are instances of pseudo-oxymoron rather than showing the logical contradiction which strictly speaking true oxymoron demands. The resulting increase in subtlety makes them no less impressive as examples of wit.

One pattern which is particularly characteristic is where a literal reading results in a violation of the expected boundaries between the four elements of earth, air, fire, and water. We may have, for example, a paradoxical clash between fire and water, as in the following references to 'wet sparks', each of which functions slightly differently.

Firstly Góngora describes the tearful Angélica's concern for the injured Medoro thus:

> Ya es herido el pedernal,
> ya despide el primer golpe
> centellas de agua. (Millé 48, lines 33-5)

In this passage we have a number of tropes working together. 'herido', 'pedernal', and 'golpe' are all metaphors, and also, probably, 'despide' where 'dismiss' is used in the sense of 'emit'. The tears shed by the hitherto unresponsive Angélica, now struck by pity, are seen in terms of sparks struck from a flintstone. Here 'centellas' is relatively abstract in concept, relying on the working out of an analogy. If you strike a flintstone you get sparks. If you metaphorically strike a metaphorical flintstone then what emerges, in this case tears, must logically be metaphorical sparks.

In the *Polifemo* the image describing Acis as sweating 'wet sparks' in the heat of a summer day (line 187) has a greater physical immediacy. The dominant factor here is the temperature. Sparks are emitted by very hot objects, and Acis is very hot. But paradoxically what emerges is wet.

Perhaps the most impressive version of the theme because of its greater degree of correspondence at the physical level is that in the *Soledades* where Góngora describes a spot

> donde la Primavera,
> --calzada abriles y vestida mayos--

centellas saca de cristal undoso
a un pedernal orlado de narcisos. (I, 576-9)

In Spring, a spring springs from a flinty rock. The bare facts become wonderfully transformed by Góngora's poetic imagination. Firstly, Spring is made the active force, the subject of the verb 'saca', which makes good sense since it is the warmer seasonal temperatures melting the snows which promotes greater vigour in the flow of water. The personification of Spring is reinforced with the subtle rather elusive metaphors describing her as shod in and clad in the months of the year in which she appears. 'Shod' suggests not only the passage of time as the months progress, but also movement and activity generally in this most active of seasons. The image 'clad' suggests the decorative blossoms characteristic of May. Since the waters emerge from a flint-stone we can again say that logically they are analogous to sparks. But there is also a physical correspondence, which completes the image, between vigorously spurting water and sparks dispersing from a point of contact. There is much harmony in this passage as well as the discord of the sparks being of water. Note, though, that for the discord to be felt at its strongest, one ideally needs to read 'cristal' as a lexicalised metaphor for water. The paradox is less immediately felt if the word 'cristal' is initially taken literally instead of being automatically read as a reference to water.

One man-made object which was frequently described in terms of a paradoxical clash between different elements in Golden-Age poetry was the ship, which Tesauro himself singles out as a source of 'il mirabile'. The classical trope for a ship of the tree easily lent itself to expressions suggesting that the ship was a creature of the land out of its element. The sails moving through the air and resembling wings or clouds also led to images of flying being applied to boats. One of Góngora's most original contributions to the repertoire of paradoxes is his description of the sailing ship as a 'vaga Clicie del viento' where the metaphorical sunflower of the ship turns with its sails to face the wind instead of the fiery sun. Another conceit offering a new twist is the description of the Victory on its voyage of discovery:

Zodiaco despues fue cristalino
a glorioso pino,
émulo vago del ardiente coche
del Sol, este elemento... (I, 466-9)

Here heaven and ocean are interchanged, giving us a correspondence between the two which is striking enough to make us rather less aware of a discordant clash. The ship progresses through its own blue expanse in an east to west direction, just like the sun. The word 'cristalino' is perfectly serviceable as a description of the sky, and so this weakens the sense of paradox which would be present if we automatically took it to mean 'aquatic'. This last example demonstrates that tropes of interchange between the four elements do not of necessity produce their sense of surprise from their seeming inappropriateness when we take them literally.

At times Góngora pairs together and counterbalances paradoxical tropes to create a figure which brings with it an added level of both harmony and discord. The description of Galatea's complexion as 'o púrpura nevada o nieve roja' is a case in point, as is that of the mixture of red and white wine in the peasants' glasses in the first *Soledad* as 'topacios carmesíes/ y pálidos rubíes' (I, 870-71). The extra element of harmony comes from the pleasing symmetry of such a pairing, but at the same time the combination of such phrases adds further tension because of our perception that when interpreting the nouns literally we would have expected the first adjective to correspond to the second noun, and the second adjective to the first noun. It is as if a switch has taken place in defiance of the normal order.

In the case of the trope of metonymy such a pairing of phrases was recognized in the classical theory of rhetoric and classified as hypallage. As Lausberg notes in his discussion of this figure, hypallage is more than a mere switch in word order, as there is a semantic shift.[77] One can demonstrate the point by observing that if one of the paired phrases is omitted, the remaining phrase still functions perfectly successfully on its own as a trope.

One of the most interesting examples of these paired images which is considerably more complex than it at first appears comes when Góngora describes the amazing swiftness of the competing runners in the first *Soledad*. It is a passage I have discussed in some detail elsewhere, but I return to it here from a slightly different perspective.[78] The young men are described as

> mancebos tan veloces,
> que cuando Ceres más dora la tierra,
> y argenta el mar desdes sus grutas hondas
> Neptuno, sin fatiga
> su vago pie de pluma
> surcar pudiera mieses, pisar ondas,
> sin inclinar espiga,
> sin violar espuma. (I, 1027-34)

Here the line 'surcar pudiera mieses, pisar ondas' contains what looks like one of the familiar switches between the elements since the verb 'pisar' would normally be expected to apply to activity on land, whilst, as Jiménez Patón pointed out, the verb 'surcar', although literally meaning 'to furrow' was a traditional dead metaphor applied to ships sailing along, a reading we opt for here in view of the inapplicability of ploughing to growing crops. The apparent interchange incidentally introduces an agreeable correspondence between cornfields and seas. Yet if we restore the words to their 'correct' order, 'pisar pudiera mieses, surcar ondas' the result remains paradoxical. Góngora seems to be describing two activities, going on foot and sailing, which both

---

[77] H. Lausberg, *Manual de retórica literaria,* translated by J. Pérez Riesco (Madrid, 1966), Vol II, pp. 144-5

[78] See *The Poet and the Natural World in the Age of Góngora* (Oxford, Oxford University Press, 1978), pp. 139-44

imply some contact with a surface, be it wet or dry, as if there were no effective contact in either case.

To trace what is happening we need to introduce a third element, namely, that of air. Góngora's paired phrases with their following qualifying adverbial phrases are in effect paradoxical descriptions of flying. The image of flying is implied by the line 'su vago pie de pluma'. Qualifying the synecdochic word 'pie', where the singular word stands for the plural, we have the double trope 'de pluma', which combines the synecdochic part/whole relationship (feather=wing) with a metonymic switch between cause and effect (wing=flight). The image of flying is reinforced a little later in the assertion 'que no pisan alas hierba', where again we have a trope in 'alas' whose literal reading produces a striking incongruity.

If Góngora's athletes were literally flying then their progress over land might be described as a kind of running and their progress over water as a kind of sailing. In what we normally think of as flying there is no surface contact with what was below, hence in a sense it becomes immaterial what the surface underneath is, and sailing and running become interchangeable as tropes for propulsion. However, Góngora goes out of his way to draw our attention to the special nature of the surfaces over which the athletes hypothetically could have 'flown'. The land-based surface is not the ground, but ears of wheat growing from it, which unlike the ground are not capable of sustaining any weight. Likewise the surface of the sea, which in any case would not support a person's weight, is described in terms of the flimsy foam which rests on top of the denser water beneath. We are thus encouraged to think in terms of surface contact between the foot and what lies beneath it, but a contact so light that not enough weight is transferred to bend an ear of corn — a kind of low flying, in fact, since if the surface which the foot contacts is not supporting any weight then the air must be.

Thus far, Góngora's paired images still leave us with an unresolved paradox. Describing running across grass in terms of a kind of low flying makes sense as a trope conveying the visual impression given by the runners. But Góngora in effect insists that the visual illusion is a reality, and that the runners could perform in the same way not only on a solid surface, but on a surface incapable of bearing weight. The trope of flying is thus taken literally, resulting in the description of a physical impossibility, whose extraordinary nature is heightened by the apparent switch between 'surcar' and 'pisar'. Either we see Góngora as depicting a world in which the normal physical laws do not apply, or we read these lines as an instance of hyperbole, in which case the simplest analysis is to take the verb 'pudiera' as a trope meaning something like 'one could easily have imagined that it could have'.

One further complication needs to be discussed before we finally leave this passage, and that is that Góngora goes on to say that no dust was thrown up by the runners:

No el polvo desparece
el campo, que no pisan alas hierba. (I, 1041-2)

Here he describes not some hypothetical situation but the physical reality at the time of the race. Are we faced once again with a potentially more puzzling impossibility? Not, I think, if we bear in mind that there may be perfectly good physical explanations of why the running feet do not throw up dust. The covering of grass binding the ground together offers a perfectly rational explanation. But Góngora wittily takes the lack of dust as a spurious 'proof' that his runners are literally flying.

Tesauro's standpoint in talking about 'Il mirabile' is that of a reader who is impressed by contradictions which emerge on a literal reading and overlooks the fact that such contradictions evaporate if one looks to the figurative meanings behind the tropes in which the seeming contradictions are explained and resolved. The assumption about the psychology of such conceits is that although the reader manages to make sense of the nonsensicality of a paradox he still retains a sharp awareness of the initial sense of surprise after the problem has been resolved.

Góngora's exaggerated description of the athletes in addition to its use of paradox illustrates how hyperbole can involve an interaction between literal and figurative readings. Hyperbole sometimes pretends to take other tropes literally, but ends up not being taken literally itself. A classic instance of this in common usage is the hyperbolic use of the adverb 'literally', as, for example, where somebody suffering from cold might say 'I was literally frozen to death'. In the following paragraphs I shall look further at the elusiveness of hyperbole, which works at the interface between the literal and the figurative.

Góngora's wonderful self-portrait poking gentle fun at his comfortable provincial lifestyle in Córdoba in the *romance* 'Ahora que estoy despacio' (Millé 8) includes fair amount of comic exaggeration. He describes himself singing in the church choir, playing cards with the mayor and chess with the priest, and writes:

> gobernaba de allí el mundo,
> dándole a soplos ayuda
> a las católicas velas
> que el mar de Bretaña surcan;
> y, hecho otro nuevo Alcides,
> trasladaba sus columnas
> de Gibraltar a Japón
> con su segundo plus ultra;
> daba luego vuelta a Flandes
> y de su guerra importuna
> atribuía la palma
> ya a la fuerza, ya a la industria;
> y con el Beneficiado,
> que era doctor por Osuma,
> sobre Antonio de Lebrija
> tenía cien mil disputas.

Arguíamos también,
metidos en más honduras,
si se podían comer
espárragos sin la bula.

Clearly very little of what Góngora says here can be literally true, but rhetorical analysis of the passage is quite tricky. There is a straightforward instance of hyperbole as trope in the wildly exaggerated 'cien mil', but the final four lines of the passage offer what we might regard as a figure rather than a trope. The comically trivial topic for discussion, ironically described as deep by the poet, seems too absurd to be credible, unless of course it was the subject of a mock discussion engaged in in jest. I prefer to see this as an exaggerated caricature of an academic theological argument the details of which we are not expected to take literally, but which serves as an illustrative pseudo-example. In these circumstances it would be inappropriate to single out individual words as instances of trope. 'Esparragos', for example, does not necessarily represent some other specific foodstuff which was talked about. Rather the whole phrase should be seen as hyperbolically figurative.

The world of armchair warfare at the start of the passage again challenges analysis. We are in a world of wishful thinking in which solutions to the nation's problems are dreamt up despite the fact that the poet has no influence whatsoever on world affairs. He is not literally 'putting the world to rights', and his geographical tour is one undertaken solely in the imagination. Thus the verbs 'gobernaba' and 'dando vuelta' can be seen perhaps as metaphoric, certainly as hyperbolic. But what are we to make of the reference to the Armada in the first four lines? Is the image of Góngora puffing in the direction of fleet a trope? Literally speaking, the poet wishes the Spanish ships every success, and perhaps speaks his mind on the subject to his companions. The 'air' of his words is perhaps not close enough to 'soplos' to provide a credible physical analogy. But merely to interpret the image in a colourless abstract fashion seems a little tame. My own response to this passage is to envisage Góngora imaginatively following through the image of 'playing God' and imagining himself having the sails of the ships under his control just as a small boy can guide a toy boat sailing in a basin with the occasional puff. On this reading what we have is not so much a trope as a figurative image which is a poetic fiction and which functions as part and parcel of a general exaggeration of the poet's ability to influence things.

Generally the distinction I am suggesting between hyperbole as figure and hyperbole as trope is that in the former case one is interpreting whole phrases, first reading them literally then toning them down, whilst in the latter case the hyperbole is seen as affecting specific words within a larger context, and these individual words are toned down by the reader while the context remains in place.

Terence May in a subtle analysis of a passage from the amoebean songs of courtship of Micón and Lícidas in the second *Soledad* recognizes some of the complex possibilities of hyperbole and sees wit in the interplay of two different levels of meaning, the plain, which is concerned with universal truths, and the rhetorical which resorts to exaggeration in pursuit of its persuasive goal. He draws attention to the incredibility at the literal, physical level of the ashes which Lícidas refers to as the result of being thunderstruck by Leusipe, or the chains which Micón cites as evidence of his enslavement to Cloris. Paradoxically, it is this rejected literal interpretation which May refers to as the rhetorical meaning, whilst the so-called plain meaning is far from plain, but involves a perception that the elusiveness of the images we attempt to grasp mirrors the impermanence of human experience at a more general level.

Lícidas:	... de tus dos soles
	fulminado ya, señas no ligeras
	de mis cenizas dieron tus riberas (II, 560-62)
Micón:	... tus prisiones ya arrastraba graves.
	Si dudas lo que sabes,
	Lee cuanto han impreso en tus arenas
	(a pesar de los vientos) mis cadenas. (II, 566-68)

May's interpretation does however gloss over some important detail in Lícidas's song. Strictly speaking, the listener is not being invited to visualise directly either the ashes or the chains, but merely the physical evidence on the sea shore which might lead us to deduce their presence. In the case of the ashes, the 'señas no ligeras', being weighty the signs clearly have to be more substantial than what might look like dispersed fragments of ash. If we envisage large boulders on the beach looking like tombstones, there we have our clue, pointing it would seem to the presence of buried ashes. In the same way indentations in the sand presumably brought about by the working of the elements are presented as proof that chains have been dragged across the shore. What is happening here, as I understand it, is that the natural phenomena of the sea shore are ingeniously offered as evidence that what we might initially have taken to be metaphors turn out to be literally true and to represent a physical reality. An extra ironic twist to the sophistry of the argument is that the wind, which is here cited as a threat to the permanence of the marks, is likely have helped to contribute to making them in the first place.

On occasion Góngora achieves a special burlesque effect by avoiding hyperbole in contexts where it might have been expected and by offering us an unexpected literalness of description. Ironically it is almost as if the avoidance of the slight vagueness of hyperbole is sufficiently deviant to constitute a figure of its own. For example, when Góngora describes Thisbe's teeth, there is wit in the accurately observed distinction between 'perlas' representing the molars and 'aljófares', which are specifically small pearls, representing the other smaller teeth. But more than this, there is a scientific accuracy in the dental count, though amusingly enough there has been some pedantic discussion as to whether Góngora was sufficiently au fait with contemporary views that women did not enjoy a full set of 32 teeth. The point is that a burlesque effect is created by the disparity between the mathematical exactness of the description and our expectation in portrayals of feminine beauty that a certain amount of flattering poetic licence will be used. The very perfection of Thisbe's teeth is a hindrance to our emotional involvement.

Another interesting example of intrusive mathematics comes at the start of one of Góngora's *romances:*

> Cuatro o seis desnudos hombros
> de dos escollos o tres
> hurtan poco sitio al mar
> y mucho agradable en él.
> Cuanto lo sienten las ondas
> batido lo dice el pie,
> que pólvora de las piedras
> el agua repetida es. (Millé 70)

The encroachment of the top of the rocks on the sea's surface is seen as a theft, which effectively personifies the rocks and encourages us to read 'desnudos hombros' as personificatory. In turn the action of the sea in beating at the submerged base of the rocks as if blasting them with gunpowder is seen as a manifestation of the sea's resentment. The dead metaphor 'pie' following as it does the image of the shoulders dies a little more as with think of an anatomical foot. But what is of particular interest at the start is the disconcerting if impeccable logic which reinforces the personification of allocating two shoulders to each rock. What is striking is the combination of vagueness in the apparent uncertainty as to how many rocks there are, and the exactness of 'cuatro o seis'. 'Two or three' is in effect an idiomatic expression meaning 'a small unspecified number' rather than 'either exactly two or exactly three'. 'Four or six' can hardly function in the same way. It is almost as if Góngora has taken literally what is an idiomatic expression. But strictly speaking although there may be doubt as to the precise number of metaphorical torsos there can be no doubt that whatever that number happens to be there will be twice as many shoulders.

The elusiveness of hyperbole as a half-way house between the literal and the figurative is matched to a large extent by the figure of personification, which basically only exists as a by-product of trope being read literally. When the accompanying tropes are understood in their figurative sense the personification in theory vanishes. Yet, as in the case of Tesauro's 'mirabile', the reader probably retains in the mind the initial impression given by a literal reading.

To take a straightforward example, when Góngora referring to the spectators' stunned reaction to the mind-boggling speed of the athletes in the first *Soledad* writes 'cojea el pensamiento' (I, 1046), the abstract word 'pensamiento' becomes personified through the use of the verb 'cojea' which can only properly apply to humans or animals. But in order to see this as a personification we have to take 'cojea' literally. If we read it as a metaphor referring to the slowness of thought then the sense of personification disappears.

Since it is only natural for us to seek first a literal meaning before looking for explanations in terms of trope many of our readings of Góngora might involve an initial literal appreciation in terms of personification later rejected in favour of a more rational alternative where tropes are recognised and understood in terms of their logical function.

That personification is the result of an interaction between different parts of an utterance taken as a whole can be seen by considering a commonplace type of metonymy, found frequently in Góngora, where a phenomenon traditionally seen as in the control of a particular classical god or goddess is referred to by the name of the deity in question. Where, for example, Góngora refers to the mixture of red and white wines served to the merrymakers as 'confuso Baco'[79] the verb 'sirvieron' of which Baco is the object does not make it likely that we will see the wine as personified, despite the fact that Baco is literally the name of a god. We are even less likely to take as a personification the reference to Atlantic and Pacific Oceans as 'un Neptuno y otro' (Soledades,II, 565), where the dead metaphor 'surca', to furrow, meaning to sail, cannot sensibly take a personal object. However, where the context tempts us into an initial literal reading which makes some sort of iconic sense then we have wit. For example, Góngora says wittily of the peasants grouped around a bonfire, 'a Vulcano tenían coronado'. He more than once uses 'coronar' as a *cultismo* for 'to encircle', given which reading 'Vulcano' emerges as a non-personificatory reference to a fire. However, we are unlikely to be able to suppress an initial reading which understands 'coronado' to mean, as it more ordinarily does, 'crowned'. On this reading 'Vulcan' is understood literally rather than metonymically, and retains his god-like identity.

Another area in which the borderline between the literal and the figurative is exploited with wit is in the treatment of 'dead' trope. The lexicalisation of a metaphor is usually something which we deduce has happened in the history of the use of a word in language, resulting in polysemy. For example, the following meanings of 'mouth' are included in Chambers' Twentieth-Century Dictionary:

1. The opening in the head of an animal by which it eats and utters sound
2. Opening or entrance, as of a bottle, river, etc.
3. A consumer of food
4. A speaker

If the first use of this word listed here happened to be the only one attested as a standard form by the lexicographers, who could be expected to pick up the commonest habits of a linguistic community, then the use of the word 'mouth' in the second sense would be read by us as a metaphor based on a resemblance between the opening of a bottle, river, etc., and the animal orifice literally referred to. The third and fourth listed uses would be read as examples of synecdoche, based on the relationship of the part to the whole. But the fact that the last three uses are given

---

79   *Soledades*, I, 868

by the lexicographers is testimony to the lexicalisation of what we assume were once examples of trope, but which are used so frequently as to have lost any sense of being deviant. Though the mouths of caves have been in existence longer than man, we assume that even for a cave-man the first meaning should be seen as the basic one, although in principle, on purely logical rather than sociological grounds, the first meaning could equally well have derived from the others.

I.A Richards' view that dead metaphor can readily be revived is one that probably would receive wide acceptance, but it should not go unchallenged, and we need to look closely at what such a revival would entail.[80]   Take our example of the lexicalised trope 'mouth of a cave', not normally perceived of as a metaphor. Firstly, nothing we do can actually de-lexicalise it.   We cannot wipe out the habits of a linguistic community and bring about cultural amnesia expunging it from our dictionaries.   And if as a result of linguistic habit it now literally refers to the entrance of a cave, this in no way differs from what it used to refer to when the metaphor was once fresh.   There is no difference in semantic function between the live and the dead trope. The difference between the two is largely aesthetic.

What is commonly thought of as the revival of dead trope ironically turns out to be the opposite. It is in fact a refusal to accept a metaphorical reading either live or dead and a substitution instead of a literal reading.   Sarbiewski very perceptively noted in his treatise that not only did wit not require the use of trope, it was often the result of the destruction of a trope through the exploitation of the literal meaning.

> Deinde tantum abest, ut metaphora aut allegoria acumen sit, ut potius in destructione allegoriae vel metaphorae acumen saepe consistat, dum verbum a translatione et sensu metaphorico ad propriam et simplicem significationem reducitur.[81]

There are striking examples of this process to be found in Góngora which merit analysis.

Describing Polyphemus's cave, he writes:

allí una alta roca
mordaza es a una cueva de su boca. (lines 31-2)

Here, to put it in crude terms, he encourages us to see the mouth of the cave as if it were literally a mouth as we respond to the metaphor of the gag.   Another way of regarding what is happening here is to see the poet as reversing the hierarchy between literal and derived meanings, taking 'opening' as the literal meaning from which a fresh metaphor, 'part of the body' is derived. A more neutral view of the process at work is to see it as more akin to a pun.   Taking a word which has multiple literal uses which vary according to context, and whose various referents relate to each in the same logical way as the literal referent relates to the effective referent in a trope, the poet uses the word in a context which requires us to read it in two senses at once.

---

80   *The Philosophy of Rhetoric*, (Oxford, 1978), p. 101
81   *De acuto et arguto, Op.cit.*,p.8.

In the case of the current example from Góngora, 'boca' remains the mouth of a cave, whilst at the same time being understood to be the mouth of a person in relation to the metaphor of the gag, which otherwise would be incomprehensible.

In characterstic fashion, for good measure Góngora follows through his idea with a later reference to the cavern as

> este formidable de la tierra bostezo

where the hyperbaton adds to the drama by keeping us waiting for the key word at the end of the line. Here the double meaning is subtly implied. We know from the context that Góngora is referring to the Polyphemus's cave, but yawning is a function of the mouths of living beings.

Another similar dead metaphor handled in an interesting way by Góngora is that of 'foot' used to refer to the base of an object. At the start of his *Polifemo* it is the foot of a cliff:

> Donde espumoso el mar siciliano
>
> el pie argenta de plata al Lilibeo

As Dámaso Alonso notes, the word 'argenta' is not pleonastic here, but is to be understood in a more specific technical sense than 'to silver' in general. The term was used to refer to the decorative application of metal work to leather as practised in particular by Andalusian shoe makers. As it applies its silver decoration to the foot of the cliff we are reminded of the shoemakers art which is used to show off human feet to advantage. The same verb is used to jocular effect in a *romancillo* in which Góngora describes the hazards faced by the would-be suitor loitering outside the house of his beloved only to be mistaken for a street corner by her dog lifting its leg.

> con gentil denueda
>
> me argentó de plata
>
> los zapatos negros (Millé 16)

A further ingenious example of a literal meaning of a dead metaphor is found in the *Soledades* where Góngora describes the foot of a tree as discourteously treading on a stream

> cuando los suyos enfrenó de un pino
>
> el pie villano, que groseramente
>
> los cristales pisaba de una fuente. (II, 317-19)

Góngora then goes on to develop the image of the stream as a spitting snake. The wit in this passage is complex. Behind the image of the spitting snake, which in turn lies behind the metaphor 'vomitando' which refers to it as a vomiting snake, we have an ingenious explanation of the cause of water being thrown into the air. Feet splashing in water achieve a effect similar to that of a suitable static obstacle placed in a swiftly flowing stream. The static base of the tree, its 'foot', functions like a moving human foot.

After the initial sharp linking of the feet of the protagonist and that of the tree which impedes his progress, simultaneously calling on two different uses of 'pie' via the word 'cuyos' in a kind of implicit syllepsis, we are encouraged to think of the foot of the tree in terms of a human foot via the words 'villano' and 'groseramente' which we expect to be applied only to human beings. These words help to produce a double personification, since both the perpetrators and victims of inconsiderateness are normally human, or at least animate in the case of the victims. 'El pie villano' turns out to be metonymic on further analysis, since it is only the tree, the controller of the foot, which could figuratively be regarded as oafish. The stream in turn is personified, which leads us smoothly into the metaphor of the serpent which Góngora goes on to develop.

In the case of this passage it is hard to assign any abstract impersonal sense to 'groseramente' that could apply to an effect brought about by the inactive base of a tree, and so we continue to read it literally and therefore to retain as a poetic fiction the image of a personified tree.

One sign of particularly sharp wit is where there are grounds for hesitation in choosing between the alternating perspectives of the literal and the figurative. A good example is found in Góngora's remarkably sharp *romance* 'Cuatro o seis desnudos hombros', which dates from 1614 and has many reminiscences of the *Soledades* which must have been very much in Góngora's mind at that time. Here the shipwrecked, lovesick noble cultivates a garden on his desert island whose red and white flowers mimic the features of his cruel beloved.

> Confusas entre los lilios
> las rosas se dejan ver,
> bosquejando lo admirable
> de su hermosura cruel
> tan dulce, tan natural,
> que abejuela alguna vez
> se caló a besar sus labios
> en las hojas de un clavel. (Millé, 70)

At first sight it looks straightforward enough. The petals of the carnation resemble red lips and the bumble bee sipping the nectar metaphorically kisses these metaphorical lips. But the words 'tan dulce, tan natural', which the context seems to indicate are best read as adverbs qualifying 'bosquejando', suggest a different perspective. The portrait in flowers is so convincing that the bee is taken in and thinks that it is a real woman. The kiss then becomes a real kiss directed at an illusory object. The degree of hyperbole which underlies the notion that a bee might be more attracted to a pair of lips than to a flower might lead us to hesitate again, perhaps resolving our reading with an acceptance of this as elegantly exaggerated praise of the extreme beauty of the girl's lips.

Where literal and figurative meanings work in harmony together a conceit is likely to be particularly memorable. This is the case where Góngora describes the view from a hilltop in the first *Soledad* using the image of a map.

> Si mucho poco mapa les despliega
> mucho es más lo que, nieblas desatando,

confunde el sol y la distancia niega. (I, 194-6)

Not only do we have the brilliant analogy between the still scrolled up part of the map and the distant heat haze but the *coup de grâce* is the perception that seen from above, the landscape is literally its own map. Mathematically speaking there is an optical mapping of the scene onto our retina.

The unusual patterns emerging from the literal treatment by the poet of commonplace tropes is effective not only in the sphere of those tropes lexicalised through the processes of everyday language, but is also exploitable in the case of those which are commonplace within a particular literary tradition. Góngora's own poetic habits and his creation of a distinctive poetic vocabulary of his own produce certain expectations in his faithful readers. Familiarity with Góngora may lead us, for example, to treat the word 'cristal' as virtually a lexicalised metaphor for water, though Dámaso Alonso's assertion that one can find no literal references to water in the *Soledades* because he always uses 'cristal' is inaccurate.[82] In fact the words 'agua' and 'aguas' appear almost exactly as many times as 'cristal' and 'cristales' in the *Soledades*.[83] Nevertheless it comes as a surprise when Góngora for once uses the word 'cristal' literally, and at the same time leads us to question whether our previous assumptions about Góngora's use of the term were correct. The shock comes when the suitor Micón, sings:

No ondas, no luciente
cristal, (agua al fin dulcemente dura)
invidia califique mi figura
de musculosos jóvenes desnudos. (II, 577-80)

we are expecting the phrase 'no luciente cristal' to be in apposition to 'ondas' as a further description of the waters, but the bracketed phrase requires us to re-think because 'dura' even when qualified by 'dulcemente' does not seem very applicable to 'ondas' in this context. Micón is asserting that he does not require the testimony of the mirror to confirm his good looks, be it the mirror of the waters, or a more solid glass mirror ('luciente cristal'). The description in parentheses establishes a correspondence between glass and water by reminding us that crystal was thought by the Ancients to have derived from water which had solidified. The two can thus be seen as chemically identical, which could undermine our whole assumption that as a trope for water 'cristal' was metaphoric. If they are made of the same substance then it could turn out to have been a synecdoche all along.

We have seen in this chapter how paradox, hyperbole, personification and lexicalized trope can all prove difficult to analyse because they can involve the reader

---

[82] In his essay 'Claridad y belleza de las Soledades', *Estudios y ensayos gongorinos* (Madrid, Gredos, 1960), p. 72

[83] See the rather hazardous concordance of A. Callejo and M.T. Pajares, *Fabula de Polyfemo y Galathea y Las Soledades. Textos y concordancia* (Madison, Hispanic Seminary of Medieval Studies, 1985), which enshrines the orthographic quirks of the Chacón manuscript.

in a subtle oscillation between literal and figurative readings. This potentially disconcerting quality lends some justification to our characterizing the wit in such cases as a kind of *discordia concors* in Sarbiewski's sense of the phrase with matches and mismatches overlaying each other.

Chapter Six: Between rhetoric and logic

In *Discurso I* of his *Agudeza y arte de ingenio*, Gracián observes that the subtleties of wit do not truly belong to the domain of rhetoric, although like orphaned children they might have been fostered by that discipline.[84]   The companion discipline to rhetoric, that of logic, also receives a mention in Discurso I.   The Ancients had rules for producing syllogisms, he notes, and so one should be able to construct conceits according to rules.[85]   However, this falls short of implying clearly that conceits should be seen as essentially logical in character.   He comes much closer to suggesting that the Ancients left the theory of wit on one side because it did not fit either rhetoric or logic:

> Hallaron los antiguos métodos al silogismo, arte al tropo; sellaron la agudeza, o por no ofenderla, o por desahuciarla, remitiéndola a sola la valentía del ingenio.

This is not to deny reasoning a vital function in the *agudeza de raciocinación*, for example, which includes conceits involving proofs and inferences.   But Gracián sees the function of that reasoning process as distinct in the fields of logic, where validity is the prime consideration, rhetoric, where persuasiveness is the main aim, and wit, where beauty reigns.

> Tiene la agudeza también sus argumentos, que si en los dialécticos reina la eficacia, en los retóricos la elocuencia, en éstos la belleza.   Usanse mucho en la poesía para exprimir y exagerar los sentidos.   Es muy ordinario dar conclusión conceptuosa a un epigrama, a un soneto, a una décima con un bien ponderado argumento. (II, 80)

Insofar as it is concerned with the art of argument, the terrain of rhetoric overlaps that of logic.   It was this overlap which led Ramus to assign the first two functions of logic according to the classical tradition, those of Invention and Disposition, to logic, and to regard rhetoric proper as encompassing Diction alone.

For our purpose the niceties of the debate about the demarcation between Rhetoric and Logic are less important than an understanding of the general principles which might lead one to categorize an aspect of an argument as something essentially logical or essentially a matter of rhetoric.   For Benedetto Croce the distinction between the two disciplines seems to primarily that of the degree of formality or

---

[84]   "...la agudeza en arte, teórica flamante, que aunque se traslucen algunas de sus sutilezas en la Retórica, aun no llegan a vislumbres: hijos guérfanos, que por no conocer su verdadera madre, se prohijaban a la Elocuencia" (I 47).

[85]   "Armase con reglas un silogismo: fórjese, pues, con ellas un concepto" (I 48).

informality. He regards what he sees as the lack of rigour in wit as aligning it with Rhetoric rather than Logic:

> The extension of the use of the term 'wit' arose from its convenience in Rhetoric as conceived by antiquity; that is to say, a suave and facile mode of knowledge as opposed to the severity of Dialectic; an "Antistrophe to Dialectic", which substituted for reasons of actual fact those of probability or fancy; enthymemes for syllogisms; examples for inductions; so much so that Zeno the Stoic figured Dialectic with her fist clenched and Rhetoric with her hand open. The empty style of the decadent Italian authors in the 17th Century found its complete justification in this theory of Rhetoric.[86]

There are a number of qualifications to be made here. Firstly Dialectic, as opposed to formal deductive logic, is concerned with the probable rather than with the necessary precisely because it is applicable in factual situations. Moreover its standards are in principle applicable to fiction, the creation of fancy. Thus a legal argument may be pursued just as well in a hypothetical case as in one drawn from real life. Secondly, there is not necessarily any difference in the standard of reasoning between an enthymeme and the corresponding syllogism. Consider the classic example of a syllogism:

All men are mortal.

Aristotle is a man.

Therefore Aristotle is mortal

The suppression of either of the two premisses or of the conclusion will produce an enthymeme, a compressed argument. But such is the redundancy in such a syllogism, with each of the three terms appearing twice, that the suppression of one of its three statements does not lead to any loss of information and the full syllogism can easily be derived from any of the three enthymemes. Clearly the compressed argument is no less valid than the full one, and one could just as well regard the enthymeme as the standard form and the syllogism as an expanded form of it.

However, there can be circumstances in literary discourse where a statement or group of statements seems to imply an argument whose precise construction or status may be dubious. We shall examine the unsettling effects of some instances of compression later. But in general terms these dubious cases mean the involvement of rhetorical considerations which disrupt the orderliness to which logic aspires. Logic purports to examine the substance of the utterances it analyses. When the language is transparent all is well. Rhetoric, on the other hand, is more concerned with the effects of the methods used to put across that substance. Where the language is complex, particularly if it is highly figurative, we may be in doubt as to what that substance is, and the logical analysis may be thrown into insecurity.

---

[86]   Benedetto Croce, *Aesthetic*, translated by D. Ainslie (London, Peter Owen, 1967), p. 189

Indeed, Croce's comments question that there is any substance behind the rhetoric of seventeenth-century wit.

Taken in their context, Croce's remarks seem to be aimed at discrediting the seventeenth-century theorists of wit whom he says 'never fail to point out that intellectual truth lies at the root of wit'. His own unsympathetic view of wit is that it is built on fancy rather than fact and its informality seems to be equated with a lack of substance, hence the concluding remark about the emptiness of seventeenth-century style.

However, the views of the theorists of wit are more varied and subtle than Croce claims. As we have seen, Gracián stresses the primacy of beauty over truth in the conceit, and Tesauro regards fallacious logic as providing the essence of the most prized conceits. And as far as the relation of wit to Rhetoric and Logic is concerned, the stance taken by Peregrini, who was not really an enthusiast of wit, was close to Croce's

> l'acutezza non consiste in un ragionamento, ma in un detto... non si regge dalla qualita della materia o del obietto significato, ma da quella dell'artificio e forma di favellare.[87]

This suggests that reasoning, coming within the terrain of logic, involves the consideration purely of the substance of what is said whilst the conceit as rhetoric is concerned basically with the medium of expression.

Peregrini backs up his view by comparing pairs of what he claims are materially identical utterances where only one member of each pair shows real wit as opposed to mere elegance.

In his later *Fonti dell'ingegno* Peregrini modifies his views to take a more balanced stance which offers a clear justification for seeing wit as having a foot in the camps of both logic and rhetoric. He distinguishes between two different aspects of wit as a faculty:

> Dico ingengo, comprendendo tanto quella parte dell'animo che, speculativa, riguarda e procura solo il vero, la quale propriamente s'appella intelletto, e ch'é governata dalla loica, quanto quella che, in un certo modo prattica, mira e cerca de trovare e di fabbricare il bello e l'efficace: la quale separatamente ritiene il commune titolo d'ingegno, e che resta del tutto in balia della retorica. ... Tocca, dico, alla loica e retorica la cura di provedere l'ingegno, benché in diversa maniera, per tutti i suoi bisogni; cioe la prima nell'inchiesta del vero, la seconda nel magistero e fabbrica dell'efficace e del bello.[88]

This balance is echoed by later theorists. It is interesting that J. Oldmixon should give his English translation of Bouhours *De la manière de bien penser dans les ouvrages d'esprit*, the title *The Arts of Logick and Rhetorick*. The Portuguese

---

87   *Trattatisti e narratori del Seicento*, p. 114

88   *ibid.*, p. 178

theorist Leitão Ferreira, a disciple of Tesauro, in the introduction to his *Nova arte de conceitos*, expresses the duality of wit more dramatically:

> Tomarey por assumpto ... hum methodo, ou arte de fabricar conceytos por imagens, & ideas engenhosas, que sera huma nova Dialectica da Poesia, huma Theoria logica da eloquencia, & huma util Rethorica [sic] da Rhetorica.

Peregrini's idea of the intellect's pursuit of truth putting it within the sphere of logic derives from the scholastic tradition of seeing logic as not limited to syllogistic reasoning but as encompassing other simpler intellectual acts. Tesauro's account of the hierarchy of different types of wit, starting with the one-word metaphor, going on to metaphorical propositions, and concluding with enthymemes based on such propositions, is modelled on the traditional view, already referred to by Peregrini and explained in more detail by Leitão Ferreira, that there are three types of operation for the intellect: simple apprehension through concepts, the processing of propositions, and finally syllogistic logic.

Strictly speaking, truth is a property neither of concepts, which assert nothing, nor of syllogisms, where validity rather than truth is the issue, but of propositions. Gracián was wise to insist that beauty rather than truth is what counts in wit once he had identified correspondences as the defining feature of wit. Correspondences are intellectually graspable relationships which are neither true nor false: they simply are. They connect things. At the level of the enthymeme it is propositions which they connect. In appreciating the ingeniousness of these connections, which may or may not involve sophistry, we will need to call on our powers of logic. In other words, the fact that we may be appreciating a kind of beauty does not in itself mean that we have strayed from the terrain of logic. However, in particular cases, as I suggested earlier, problems in interpreting a complex text may make secure logical analysis difficult.

An insight into this problem can be obtained by reflecting on Tesauro's extension of the concept of the enthymeme to include what he calls 'laconic conceits' which offer enthymemes only in outline form. If we accept his view that the more succinct the conceit the wittier, then presumably the sharpest of all ought to be those without any expressed verbal content at all drawn from the world of visual art. He cites as an example of one such 'argomento poetico' an emblem picturing Achilles as a lion:

> La Pittura intende di farti credere, che il finto sia vero: & la metafora, che Achille sia un Leone. Il che si conchiude con vn Parologismo di tre Affermatiue in Seconda Figura: cioe; *Il Leone e feroce e Achille e feroce: Dunque Achille e vn Leone.*

The example is not a felicitous one, not least because it lacks wit. Secondly, it is virtually impossible to discuss without some inkling as to how the connection between Achilles and the Lion is represented visually. Is it merely a case of a picture of a lion bearing on it an inscription identifying it as Achilles? However, the logic which Tesauro sees as implied here could presumably be regarded as present in any verbal metaphor. But what Tesauro offers here is an author's eye view. A reader might approach the logic thus:

> Achilles was not a lion but a man; but he did resemble a lion in his ferocity; therefore when the author says he is a lion he must mean that he is like a lion.

A more fruitful example taken from painting will illustrate how doubts about the interpretation of what we see lead to insecurity in identifying the underlying logic.

The painting I have chosen is René Magritte's *Les promenades d'Euclide* which offers a view from an upstairs window.[89] Immediately in front of the window is placed an easel on which there is a canvas depicting a scene which we assume corresponds exactly to the view from the window and which merges perfectly with the view seen through the remainder of the window which is not obscured by the canvas. On the left of the picture on the canvas there is a conical turret whose tip is aligned exactly with the horizon. On the right is a road stretching into the distance which converges to a point at the horizon, and exactly matches the turret in shape. There is wit in the unexpected correspondence between the two, and, we suspect, an artistic fallacy. Could such a parity of appearance between tower and road have presented itself to an observer situated in such a room? The exact fit between the scene on the canvas and the surrounding view through the window invites us to conclude that the artist has faithfully copied what stood in front of him. Is Magritte offering us a satire on the conventions of perspective? And what role in the argument is played by the ocular adjustment that would be required to focus on a canvas inside a room and then on the scene outside the room stretching into the distance, bearing in mind that Magritte represents both the canvas and the outside view upon the single plane of his own canvas? In a case like this logical considerations interact with 'rhetorical' ones which focus on the medium of expression and the issue of what exactly is being represented. In the case of an artist like Escher, logic may be forced to give up when what is 'represented' may be logically incapable of existing in the real world and may rely on optical illusion.

Tesauro's discussion of the enthymeme encompasses some interesting marginal cases. There are examples of what he calls the 'metafora di decettione' which rely on non-sequiturs so blatant that we have merely the form of an argument instead of an actual argument.[90] Presumably these do not count as enthymemes at all. But more interesting is the case of observations involving a kind of non-deductive thinking which Tesauro concedes is not strictly enthymematic, but which he claims has a vague appearance of being so. This process involves a reflection on two circumstances of the subject of discourse, when there exists between them some

---

[89]   For a reproduction of this painting, see Suzi Gablik, *Magritte* (London, Thames and Hudson, 1976), plate 67.

[90]   'Non sono argomenti & simigliano argomenti' *Il Cannocchiale Aristotelico* (Torino, 1670), p. 472

proportion or disproportion: which is mainly used in conceits founded on opposition or the marvellous.[91]

The example he gives is a Latin epigram about an ant enclosed in a piece of amber, of which it is said that though it was despised in life, the ant has become precious in death. Although Tesauro offers no further analysis, his view might well have been that in a case like this what could be regarded as suppressed is some proposition to the effect that one would have expected the ant to be of even less value when dead than when alive. The 'conclusion', which is not strictly speaking a logical deduction, is the observation that the circumstances of this ant's death defy our expectations. Another way of analysing this in deductive terms would be to say that the following argument is implied: living creatures are of more value than dead creatures; this ant was of little value when alive; therefore this ant is even more worthless now dead. In the epigram, not only is the first premiss suppressed, but so is the conclusion, to be replaced with a new 'conclusion' that the ant is precious, which contradicts the suppressed conclusion as to its worthlessness. The contradiction is explicable as being the result of the fallacy of equivocation in that what was despised in life and what is prized in death are not the same thing. It was the ant alone which was despised in life, but it was the combination of both ant and amber which was admired after the insect's death.

Thus far we have seen some of the complexities and difficulties of practical logical analysis where an argument seems to be implied but is not spelled out. Before we face the challenge posed by some of Góngora's ingenious arguments it is worth considering whether the concept of argument can legitimately be extended, as some have suggested, to encompass poetic imagery in general.

Rosemond Tuve in her study of Elizabethan and Metaphysical imagery justifies the view that images are a type of argument with reference to the theorists' recommendation that poets make use of the Places, or Topics as they are alternatively known, as an aid to invention. The topics, described by Cicero as 'the bases of arguments' ('sedes argumenti'), belonged to that part of rhetoric which overlapped with logic and which was assigned solely to the realm of logic by Ramus.

Although the Topics can be used to produce propositions and fully fledged arguments, as a set of prompts they could equally point to different types of trope in isolation from any proposition which one might wish to form using such tropes. Thus the trope of synecdoche might be derived from the Topics of 'genus' or 'species', or metonymy from those of 'causes' or 'effects'. Although these tropes might conceivably lead a writer or a reader to produce an argument along the lines suggested above, in relation to Tesauro's example concerning the metaphor of Achilles being a lion, it is stretching a point to claim that the tropes actually comprise such an argument. The tropes do however rely on the intellectual grasping of a relationship. This makes them a the broad sense logically based in that they rely on

---

91   *Op.cit.*, 498

conceptualisation, on the *logos*. They depend on what was thought of in scholastic
terms as the first operation of the intellect rather than the syllogistic reasoning which
constituted the third operation of the intellect.

Rosemond Tuve ventures the opinion that the metaphysical conceit is
characterised by the multiplicity of its logical bases, so that it might be produced by
the use of several of the Places at once.[92] Of the theorists of wit, it is Sarbiewski,
with his threefold method of using the Ciceronian Topics, who comes closest to
demonstrating what this might mean in practice.

The first method advocated by him is to

> 'compare the subject matter itself with the rhetorical topics, and
> investigate what the definition of this thing is, what are its parts, its
> etymology, its genus, its opposite, and what resembles it. From this
> comparison the nexus between matching and mis-matching elements can
> easily be discovered.[93]

He gives as an example from the Topic 'enumeration of parts' Seneca's statement that
the world on which man sails, goes to war, and rules is but a point, where the mismatch is provided by the disparity of trying to envisage the listed activities of man
being carried out on a point which has no size.

The second procedure is

> 'if we compare the Topics relating to the subject matter with other
> Topics, not of the same order, but of a different one, e.g. comparing the
> Topic 'definition' not with 'definition', but with   'effects' or some such
> other different Topic. '[94]

He illustrates this from the description of Lucretia by Valerius Maximus as having a
virile soul which by misfortune was assigned to a female body. Sarbiewski sees this
as derived from a comparison between material and formal causes, which for the
purposes of his argument counts as an example derived from Topics of a different
order, since material and formal causes are conceptually distinct.

Finally, Sarbiewski envisages the comparison between Topics of the same order,
as in the following example which is said to compare cause with cause and effect
with effect which says of Rome and the Tiber:

> 'quae sunt immota labascunt,et quae perpetuo sunt agitata, manent.[95]

---

92   Rosemond Tuve, *Elizabethan and Metaphysical Imagery* (Chicago, University of
        Chicago Press, 1947), p. 264

93   'si materam ipsam fonceramus com locis oratoriis et investigemus, quenam sit
        definitio huius rei, que partes, quae notatio, quod genus, quod contrarium, quod
        simile, ex qua collatione facile invenietur in re proposita nexus dissentanei et
        consentanei', *De acuto et arguto*, p. 12

94   'si ipsius materiae locos comparemus cum aliis locis non eiusdem ordinis, sed
        divefs, v.g. definitionem non cum definitione, sed cum effectis, sed cum causis vel
        aliis cum locis diversi ordinis.', *Op.cit.*, 13.

95   'Thing which are motionless wear away: those which are for ever moving survive',
        Op.cit., 14

If we look at these examples of Sarbiewski's from the reader's point of view it is clear that merely trying to identify the Topics on which they are based does not go very far in explaining what is happening logically in these passages and that there is not always any single definitive way of analysing the logic of these conceits. For instance, Gracián would probably have analysed the last example in a quite different way from Sarbiewski.

Gracián's account of how the *agudeza de semejanza* is produced suggests how he might have explained this example:

> En este modo de conceptear caréase el sujeto, no ya con sus adyacentes propios, sino con un término extraño, como imagen, que le exprime su ser, o le representa sus propiedades, efectos, causas, contingencias, y demás adjuntos [96]

By referring to the term of comparison as external Gracián preserves the idea that the discourse has a single main subject. However, from the point of view of the operation of the Topics it is as if there were two separate subjects, each with its own set of Topics. The implication is that the subject of discourse is not some general theme, but a particular item on which our attention is focussed possibly as part of the development of a broader theme. Thus in the case of Sarbiewski's example about Rome and the Tiber, Gracián might have regarded 'Rome' as being the principal subject rather than some general theme of permanence or impermanence, and the Tiber as the 'external term' with which it is being compared. In Sarbiewski's example, since the two are being contrasted the result is a conceit of dissimilarity rather than of similarity. The Topic of 'consequents' could be applied to each to bring out the contrasting pattern. But Sarbiewski, interestingly enough, saw the Topics of cause and effect as being at work here, a point of view which assumes that the reader falls for the invalid conclusion 'post hoc ergo propter hoc' which is hinted at but not overtly stated. It is not Rome's immobility which caused it to crumble or the Tiber's mobility which caused it to endure, but we are invited to envisage a topsy-turvy world in which the expected cause/effect mechanism is ironically reversed.

Because what constitutes the subject of discourse can be specified at varying levels of generality the possibility is opened up of applying the techniques of invention at different levels. It may be that the application of the theory of topics as envisaged by the theorists of wit operates at a more detailed level than was envisaged by rhetoricians in the classical mould. Peregrini's argument that wit is more a question of presentation than substance relies on a broad interpretation of what constitutes the subject matter of an utterance which is at loggerheads with the narrower interpretation implied by Gracián. He contends, for example, that a facial description in which Statius describes the ruddy cheeks of the young Achilles contrasting with the surrounding fair skin in terms of 'fire among the snow' has the same subject matter

---

[96]   *Obras completas, Op.cit.,*

as a some lines by Ovid about Venus's reluctance to take a good-looking companion to heaven with her in case Mars showed an interest.[97] True, the general subject is that of physical beauty, but the thought processes involved at a more detailed level are obviously radically different. In this respect it seems perverse to claim that it is merely the presentation and not the substance which separates both examples. One could also challenge Peregrini's opinion that it is only the second of these two examples which shows wit, as the logical opposition between the heat of fire and the coldness of snow provides a correspondence which arguably shows wit.

The objection that Peregrini is not comparing like with like could equally well apply to any comparison whatsoever between a figurative statement incorporating trope and what might be regarded as its equivalent in literal terms. To take an example from Góngora, when he refers to animals slaughtered in the hunt as 'giving foaming coral to the river Tormes', from the standpoint of classical rhetorical theory what he has done is opt for the 'decorative' word 'coral' instead of the literal term 'blood'. The subject matter in both instances would be seen as the flowing of blood into the river, and the difference between the two would be seen as a question of diction, of presentation. But such an analysis fails to recognize the relationship of similarity between blood and coral, and completely fails to cope with the correspondence, on which the wit of this phrase is based, between coral and water. From the classical standpoint, it would have made no difference if Góngora had opted for the metaphor 'rubies' instead of 'coral', but from the standpoint of the theory of wit the logical substance of what is said is completely changed.

The theory of Topics, then, whatever its links with logic in the broad sense, offers a rather blunt tool with which to dissect conceits, and relies for its application on our being able to identify what the subject of discourse is where there may be more than one candidate.

In selecting the illustrations from Góngora in this chapter I shall concentrate on conceits which Gracián would probably have classified as 'agudezas de raciocinación' or as 'agudezas de ponderación juiciosa sutil' offering or inviting explanations of problematic phenomena. This is because Góngora's exploitation of the interface between rhetoric and logic has effectively already been illustrated in Chapter Five where we saw the kind of rational exploration stimulated in the reader by Góngora's rhetorical technique of straddling the literal and the figurative. In this chapter, therefore, we shall concentrate on the more purely logical aspect by focussing on cases where the overt form is that of an argument, albeit a compressed one.

It is worth noting at the outset that not all overt arguments will necessarily contain the kind of wit for which we are looking. A poem of courtship, such as the love song addressed by Góngora's Polifemo to Galatea, is obviously an exercise in persuasion which may embody a number of conceits without necessarily becoming an *agudeza de raciocinación* as opposed to a rhetorical argument. For it to be

---

[97] *Trattatisti e narratori del seicento*, pp. 115-6

categorized as such there has to be wit in the actual logic of the argument. In practice this often means that it has to use a reasoning process which is plausible enough not to seem stupid — therein lies its beauty — but which is at the same time transparently fallacious. Tesauro describes such an argument as 'an urbanely fallacious enthymeme', distinguishable from arguments which use sophistry with the serious intention of misleading others in that we are expected to see through the trickery and enjoy the logical manœuvering which lies behind it.

However, fallaciousness is not an absolute requirement for an argument to show wit in its logic. The wit of some arguments relates as much to their structure as to the validity or otherwise of their reasoning. This is typically the case with interactive arguments, whether in real life or on the stage, where a speaker's words may thrown back at him or her in a retort or an *ad hominem* argument. The wit comes in the ingenious adaptation of speaker A's words by speaker B to pursue a quite different and possibly opposite case.

For example, much enjoyment is to be had from the witty sparring involving Tadeo in Góngora's comedy, much appreciated by Gracián, *Las firmezas de Isabela*. Witness the following interchange:

Camilo.	Qué has pronosticado hoy?
Tadeo.	Que es muerte servir dos amos;
	porque esto de ser de a dos
	no es sino para reales.
Isabela.	Y para doblones tales
	como lo habéis sido vos.
Tadeo.	Yo doblón?
Isabela	Y de dos caras.
Tadeo.	Si tengo cara detrás
	un ojo tendrá no más
Laureta	¡Así de los dos cegaras! (lines 1170-1180)

Tadeo, emphasising the difficulty of serving two masters at once, jokes that being split two ways is a fate appropriate only to the *real*, as a coin of the realm. Isabela puns that Tadeo is a dubloon, a word which as the augmentative form of 'doble' can function as an adjective meaning 'pronouncedly double'. The pun is further developed with the comment that as a 'doblón' Tadeo is two-faced, which corresponds to the idea of a two-headed coin. Tadeo replies that if he has a face at the back as well as at the front then it can have only one eye. Laureta comes back with an insult which extends the logical implications of Tadeo's joke. The 'eye' in his backside is a blind one, and Isabela expresses the wish that he will be similarly blinded in the two seeing eyes of his face. The argument pursues its seamless course, continuing beyond this extract as each character responds to the other, adding new correspondences at every turn.

Although, technically speaking, *ad hominem* arguments are logically invalid, we are impressed by their rhetorical force, and in an interchange such as the above we are much more aware of the ingenious adaptability of the characters as they link their words to what has gone before than of the possible invalidity of their case.

In conceits based on deductive arguments, however, the key often does lie in the fallaciousness of the reasoning. Here it is interesting to consider what gets suppressed in the reasoning process, and in what way the logic seems to be fallacious.

A clear case of playful sophistry can be found in Góngora's description of an island in his second *Soledad*:

> cuya forma tortuga es perezosa:
> díganlo cuantos siglos ha que nada
> sin besar de la playa espaciosa
> la arena, de las ondas repetida. (II, 192-5)

The first slightly slippery piece of logic here is the smuggling in of the adjective 'perezosa' which is not properly applicable to the shape of anything. But we may perhaps interpret the word 'forma' here as a metonym for 'appearance'. Again the description of the turtle as lazy rather than slow might be seen as false logic, in that proof of slowness is not tantamount to proof of laziness. On the other hand it could simply be taken to mean 'slow' if we read it metonymically. Where undoubtedly Góngora cheats with his logic, however, is in the witty justification of the adjective on the grounds that the island's failure to reach the nearby mainland despite the elapse of centuries offers proof of its sluggishness. The implicit argument is along these lines:

> The more slowly or lazily one swims the less progress one makes through the water; this island has failed to cross the short stretch of water separating it from the mainland despite the elapse of hundreds of years; therefore insofar as this island is like a turtle, it is like a very lazy turtle.

From the fact that laziness results in slow progress it does not logically follow that a lack of progress through water is evidence of lazy swimming. The sophistry at work here is very similar to that found in the joke:

> "Why are you carrying that umbrella on such a fine day?"
> "It's to keep the elephants away."
> "But there aren't any elephants in this country."
> "Yes. Effective, isn't it?"

In Góngora's example, the trickery comes with the slipping in of the verb 'nada'. We start off with 'la tortuga' being not a metaphor, but a term of comparison. Almost imperceptibly we drift into a territory half way between metaphor and literal language with the verb. Metaphorically the turtle-shaped island is swimming, or at least treading water, in that it keeps itself partly above the surface of the water. But it is not literally swimming, and the analogy behind the metaphor breaks down if we envisage swimming as involving propulsion through the water. But for the purposes of his argument Góngora suppresses the information that there is no visible forward movement, and draws consequences which only follow if the island were literally swimming and moving forward. No doubt if Góngora relied on the idea that some geological movement in the earth's crust were in fact moving the island towards the mainland a minuscule amount at a time then we would have more of a problem in seeing through his sophistry. But even here we would have a divergence between the appearance of things as presented to the senses and what we know intellectually to be the case where that goes beyond what is presented to our eyes. However we dress the facts up, the island does not appear to the observer to be moving at all, and to suggest on this basis that it appears to be lazy is to use a flawed logic.

One further subtlety in the description of the island which enhances the conceit is the traditional view of the tortoise as a very slow creature. In Spanish the same word, 'tortuga' is used for the land-based creature and its no doubt swifter aquatic counterpart. The justification for the adjective 'perezosa' is therefore reinforced if we allow ourselves to succumb to the false logic of using the term 'tortuga' in two different senses in the implied fallacious enthymeme: Tortugas [land-based] are notoriously slow; therefore if this island is a tortuga [aquatic] it must be slow.

Another instance in which fallacious intellectually based conclusions are allowed to overrule the evidence of the senses is found in the following sonnet (Millé 220), which despite its early date is a poem of remarkable formal perfection.

> O claro honor del líquido elemento,
> dulce arroyuelo de corriente plata
> cuya agua entre la yerba se dilata
> con regalado son, con paso lento,
>
> Pues la por quien helar y arder me siento
> Mientras en ti se mira, Amor retrata
> de su rostro la nieve, y la escarlata
> en tu tranquilo y blando movimiento,
>
> Vete como te vas. No dejes floja
> la undosa rienda al cristalino freno
> con que gobiernas tu veloz corriente
>
> Que no es bien que confusamente acoja
> tanta belleza en su profundo seno
> el gran señor del húmedo tridente.

In an argument whose structure follows that of the verse form, the poet addresses the stream in the first quatrain, describing its clarity and the gentleness of its flow, describes in the second quatrain how the beautiful face of the poet's beloved is reflected in its waters, goes on to make a request, in view of this, that the stream should continue to flow slowly and restrain its pent up power, and in the final tercet explains the reason for the request, namely, that it would be inappropriate for Neptune to receive into his bosom a blurred portrait of such a beauty. One part of the argument is obviously that a turbulent torrent is incapable of providing a clear reflection, but what is sharp in the conclusion of the poem is the tacit assumption that Neptune, the sea god, receives not only the waters of the stream as they flow into the sea, but also the image reflected in their silvery surface. This assumption depends on a tacit argument which though clearly wrong is none the less plausible. Although visual observation of streams reveals no such process happening, none the less the question poses itself that if the reflection appears to be situated within the water, and if the water clearly flows to the sea, then what is there to prevent the image itself being borne away?

In a sense this conceit is the opposite counterpart to certain others of Góngora in which we are encouraged to accept what our senses tell us rather than our intellect. Here it is the plausible though incorrect reasoning of the intellect which, if we accept it, overrides the evidence of our senses. We do not see the reflection flow away, though we reason that it must do. But an alternative analysis would make this another case of sensory deception. The reflection appears to be in the water, but physically speaking it is not, and the image is a virtual one. Since it is not really there, clearly it cannot flow away. But our eyes tell us that it is there.

There is another striking conceit in the above sonnet which relies purely on the placing of certain words to imply a relationship which is never stated. The apparent circumlocution to refer to the beloved as 'la por quien helar y arder me siento' is far from otiose because the two verbs 'helar' and 'arder' match with perfect symmetry the two nouns describing the white and red colours of the girl's complexion — 'de su rostro la nieve y la escarlata'. Just as real snow makes us physically cold, so we have a hint that the metaphorical snow of the girl's skin is to be seen as causally linked to the metaphorical coldness felt by the lover. The fiery scarlet colour can then correspondingly be linked to the heat of passion. This is far from being an overt argument, but none the less it can be analysed in terms of a tacit reasoning process which is rather subtler than a false argument in which there is an illegitimate attempt to argue from a figurative premiss to a literal conclusion. Rather than arguing that metaphorical snow can make one literally cold, the poet shows a match between a figurative cause and a figurative effect achieved by reference to the literal meaning of the terms involved.

Another remarkable poem of Góngora's is a *canción* of 1600, 'Qué de invidiosos montes' (Millé 388), which could well be a wedding song, although its shocking intimacy does presuppose a rather special relationship with the happy couple. Presenting himself as a jealous exiled suitor of the bride, the poet states that despite the formidable geographical obstacles separating him from the beloved, his thought knows no boundaries and cannot be prevented from observing jealously her new husband's activities as a lover. What give the poem its voyeuristic flavour is the poetic fiction which describes the process of seeing with the mind's eye as if it consisted of direct visual observation. The trick is achieved by picturing the imagination as a winged being conquering all obstacles as it makes its way to the nuptial chamber, swoops down over the four-poster bed, and peers within its curtains.

There is irony in the separation between the poet and his own imagination that results from this as his thought is instructed to fly off and bring back news of what it sees. Despite the theme that the imagination is completely free to do as it wants, by equating imagination with direct observation Góngora imposes limits of space and time on it, as if to witness a particular event it has to travel to the right place at the right time, and that in the meantime the poet must wait for it to return. The sharpest irony of the poem then comes from the poet's complaint that his thought has arrived too late to witness the newly-weds in the throes of lovemaking.

> Tarde batiste la invidiosa pluma,
> que en sabrosa fatiga
> vieras (muerta la voz, suelto el cabello)
> la blanca hija de la blanca espuma
> no sé si en brazos diga
> de un fiero Marte o de un Adonis bello;
> ya anudado a su cuello
> podrás verla dormida,
> y a él casi trasladado a nueva vida.

Here we see Góngora imagining the very scene which his imagination is accused of having missed. The details, though incomplete, are suggestive, with the stifled voice and the hair let down conveying a sense of ecstatic abandon. The poet's stratagem has the cunning of the rhetorical figure of *retentio* where a speaker enumerates all things which he is not going to mention in praise or blame of his subject, thereby mentioning them in the process. And so Góngora has his cake and eats it, demonstrating the true liberty of the imagination, even capable of imagining a representation of itself, whilst he pretends at the same time that it has some of the limitations of direct perception.

Although this last example does not outwardly take the form of a logical argument, it is, like the previous ones, based on a deception, in this case where the poet pretends that he is not doing the very thing which he is doing. Ultimately the wit lies in subtle logical inconsistencies in the various statements which he makes.

But it is worth noting here a pair of very similar conceits from the *Soledades* in which an overt logical slant is put on the poetic image. In one the spot where some peasant girls relax on the grass is described as an

> espacio breve
> en que, a pesar del sol, cuajada nieve,
> y nieve de colores mil vestida,
> la sombra vió florida
> en la hierba menuda. (I, 625-9)

The argument is that whereas snow can normally be expected to melt rather than settle when the sun is shining, this snow nevertheless manages to settle on the grass. The flaw behind this *ponderación de dificultad*, as no doubt Gracián would have called it, is that the restriction applies only to literal snow, and not to the figurative snow of the girls' limbs.   Compare the description in the second *Soledad* of the flowers near a group of poplar trees as 'lilios, que en fragantes copos/ nevó el mayo, a pesar de los seis chopos' (II, 335-6). Here the idea is that the trees might normally protect the ground beneath them from falling snow, but that this snow has apparently defeated this protection.

In the case of the kind of examples we have been looking at we are in the world of dialectics in which demonstration is based on the assessment of probabilities. Although sometimes the logic may be formally flawed by illicit procedures, such as the use of the same term in different senses, at other times what is at issue is more the truth or otherwise of the implied or overt propositions on which the argument is based. The argument may be flawed because it relies on bad physics rather than bad logic. The reader is in a situation not dissimilar from that of somebody trying a case in a court of law and weighing up in practical terms how far the evidence supports one interpretation of events or another. And with wit as with the law one is using one's powers of reasoning to arrive at an assessment of what significance underlies the rhetoric in which the case is presented.

Chapter Seven: Never mind the quality, feel the wit?

General descriptions of the nature of the conceit from the very fact that they are general will fit examples which we may think of as outstanding, and others which we may regard as mediocre. How low the standard can sink before we judge that we are dealing with a failed attempt at wit is going to depend to a fair degree on personal taste. Nevertheless, even in those cases which we are happy to regard as genuine conceits, there will be some which impress us more than others. To explain the difference in perceived quality we need to look for distinguishing features in a series of examples which may all have the common property of being based on logical correspondences. The theorists of wit in singling out certain specific types of conceit for praise or blame provide a starting point for examining the issue.

When it comes to those kinds of conceit most prized by the various theorists, the question of decorum is a recurrent problem. For example, Gracián is enthusiastic about what he calls the *agudeza de ponderación juiciosa sutil*, which, as we have already seen, involves the expression of a correspondence in a heightened form, and includes conceits involving exaggeration, and paradox. Clearly it would be possible to exaggerate to such an extreme degree that the result seems ridiculous, and decorum is threatened. Gracián is no doubt aware of this when he states that exaggeration is unacceptable unless it is well founded,[98] and the requirements of judiciousness and subtlety imply a further restriction on the artist. The tension involved in paradox in particular may produce an incongruous effect which is extreme enough to seem absurd, producing a similar breach in decorum. George Williamson has noted that the potential problem of a disconcerting effect being produced by the 'discordia concors' of wit which sees likeness in the unlike, which leads him to see the burlesque as the natural home for the tensions of the conceit. Yet the case of Góngora who was at home in so many different genres shows that although paradox could be exploited to comic effect in burlesque poems, such as the *Romance de Píramo y Tisbe* (Millé 74), where decorum is deliberately sacrificed, it was also quite compatible with a touching lyricism as in the highly paradoxical *romance* concerning two different lovers, Angélica and Medoro (Millé 48).

Peregrini's view that the more remote the objects connected by wit the stronger the wit again poses the problem that what his theory identifies as the most

---

[98]   'Requiérese, pues, que alguna circunstancia especial dé motivo y ocasión al encarecimiento para que no sea libremente dicho, sino con fundamento, que es darle alma al concebir', *Op.cit.*, 326

praiseworthy of conceits could in practice involve a disparity so extreme that the effect is spoiled. As for Tesauro's praise of the 'urbanely fallacious argument' as the truest form of wit, the playfulness implicit in its deception of the reader in a way which he is expected to see through might seem to be out of place in a serious poem.

What these considerations suggest is that the general formal structure of the theoretically most prized kinds of conceit is not sufficient to guarantee their success, since the same structure may be shared by conceits which attract little admiration because they seem out of place. The comments of some theorists and critics imply that the difference between success and failure depends on questions of quantity or of degree rather than of principle. Judgment of when the mark has been overstepped can then easily become reduced to a matter of the personal tastes and prejudices of the individual.

For example, the excessive striving for the extraordinary, or the recondite, an important general ingredient of wit, may according to the conservative minded Pedro de Valencia be precisely what creates the wrong emotional effect in the reader, and leave an impression of immaturity. Again, Peregrini, who shares many of the prejudices of Pedro de Valencia, states that used in excessive quantity wit becomes mere buffoonery, an argument which relies on the false premise that wit perforce contains an element of frivolity. He also tries his hand at identifying specific categories of sub-standard conceit ('acutezze vitiose'), including 'cold' conceits, caused by excessive exaggeration. In other words, these latter conceits are flawed by an excess of the quality which used judiciously was admired by Gracián in the *agudeza de ponderación*.

Just as excess is identified by theorists as one potential cause of failure, so the converse flaw of deficiency plays a part in the theories, where the artist is seen as failing to provide some desired ingredient. Sometimes the same material may be looked at from either of these two opposite perspectives, but one may be more helpful than the other. For example, the accusation that a particular comparison is too far-fetched is hard to justify convincingly. The 'remoteness' of objects or the 'distance' between them is not measurable. And arguments about likeness and unlikeness can easily become circular. Johnson said of the metaphysical poets that their images were often 'far fetched but worth the carriage', implying that they work satisfactorily despite being far fetched. If we change our perspective and see conceits in terms of their degree of connectedness, analysis becomes much easier. To say that a conceit is too remote may be merely a less helpful way of observing that its elements are insufficiently connected to be convincing, and that it lacks any beautiful correspondence.

In an article in 1953, S. L. Bethell insisted on the importance of the remoteness of the terms in a conceit rather their logical links as the distinguishing feature of wit.[99] He opposed Rosemond Tuve's contention that "our reactions really depend on the aptness of the logic by which the terms are connected", and claimed that both Tesauro and Gracián define wit as a binding together of the remote.

Bethell's argument is not helped by the fact that Gracián's famous definition of the *concepto* as 'un acto del entendimiento que exprime la correspondencia que se halla entre los objectos' makes no mention of remoteness, but places the weight on *correspondencia*. Gracián's wisdom in adopting this perspective becomes apparent when we try to analyse what might constitute excessive remoteness. Do contradictories, for example, illustrate the maximum degree of remoteness? If so, the fact that many paradoxical conceits, notably in Góngora, work perfectly well suggests that failure in other cases could not be attributable simply to extreme remoteness. Or should we regard as more remote objects which we simply would not think of connecting? What about, for example, the famous analogy made by Donne between two lovers and a pair of compasses in his poem *A Valediction* ? In a case like this the importance of the degree of connectedness established by the poet becomes clear if we consider how a reader might react to other ways of talking about the same terms. For example, a bald statement without further explanation that lovers are like compasses would clearly not be regarded as a conceit. Again the establishment of a minimal connection between the two, such as the bald observation that they both have legs would be hardly likely to impress. Ultimately our reaction is determined not by our unaided sense of the arbitrariness or otherwise of connecting these objects, but upon how impressed we are by the links actually made by the poet.

In the following paragraphs I shall consider further the problems of pinning down alleged excessiveness in the conceit before turning later in the chapter to look at failure from the point of view of deficiency.

The specific issue of how readers respond to exaggeration highlights the complexity of value judgments about whether particular conceits are flawed by excess. The following specific examples from Góngora's *Soledades* are instructive.

Juan de Jáuregui in his amusing attack on Góngora's poem singled out a number of examples of hyperbole for adverse criticism:

> Algunas exageraciones usa Vm. tan disformes i desproporcionadas, que no se pueden conportar, como llamar a la cecina de macho:
> Purpureos hilos es de grana fina.
> Al pabo negro, siendo ave grosera, le nombra VM.:
> ... Esplendor de el Occidente.[100]

These first two examples would probably not have been included by a modern reader on a list of Góngora's overstatements. In the first, Jáuregui does not specifically identify the objectionable feature, but probably it is the description of the colour of

---

99   S. L. Bethell, 'Gracián, Tesauro and the nature of Metaphysical wit', in *A Northern Miscellany of Literary Criticism,* (Manchester, 1953), pp. 19-40

100   *Documentos gongorinos*, ed. E.J. Gates, (Mexico, Colegio de México, 1960), p. 122

the meat rather than its disintegration during the cooking process to mere strands of meat. Read literally, the two colour words 'purple' and 'cochineal' refer to specific shades of red either of which may seem too bright or rich to be a likely colour for cooked meat without the use of extra colouring in the culinary process. We are at the borderline here between metaphor, the trope of resemblance, where the colour of the meat might be said to resemble that of purple, and synecdoche, where a specific type of red is used to refer to red colour as a genus. We are also at the borderline between living and dead, lexicalised trope, in that Góngora so habitually uses 'purpúreo' to refer to red things that it becomes a part of his poetic vocabulary. In order for us to see Góngora's description as exaggerated we would need to be sharply aware of the literal sense of his words, and regard the literal reading as an overstatement of the 'true' colour.

In replying to the second example concerning the turkey, Díaz de Rivas argues in reply that there were plenty of precedents for the use of the term 'esplendor' to refer not literally to physical radiance but to denote something outstanding.[101] In other words, here is another case of what is in effect lexicalised trope which read as such is unlikely to make us feel that the writer is exaggerating. However, one suspects that Jáuregui's point does not just concern the colour of the bird, but also that he regards such an 'ave grosera' as unworthy of praise. Díaz de Rivas shifts the grounds of the argument to the excellence of the turkey as a source of meat from that of its physical appearance, quite rightly, since the poet himself states that the bird is 'no bello' (310).

Jáuregui continues a little later:

> En todas las serranas encarece Vm. la belleza por un mismo nivel, hora sea la
> novia, hora la gallegota que ordeñó las vacas.
>
> De rústica vaquera,
> blanca, hermosa mano, cuyas venas
> la distinguieron de la leche apenas.

In this example we need to distinguish between different types of exaggeration. Firstly the implication of Jáuregui's comment that at the general level rather than the level of this particular expression there are too many beauties depicted, an argument which fails to impress Díaz de Rivas. Clearly, since Góngora has not set his poem in an identifiable geographical location he is at perfect liberty to depict a community whose complexion and features may be unusual.

Secondly, there is an issue as to whether in general it is appropriate to ascribe conventionally prized female pallor to peasants. As Francisco de Córdoba puts it:

---

101   'El Antítodo se maravilla por qué llama nuestro Poeta esplendor del Occidente, siendo ave negra, y no advirtió que es galana fase llamar esplendor lo que adorno, ennoblece e ylustra, aunque sea negro o blanco. ..Luego, eruditamente habló nuestro Poeta, pues el pabo de las Indias es la más excelente ave para las mesas; y entre los Romanos tuvo el mismo lugar el pabo real'. Gates, *loc.cit.*, n. 69

'No sé que se halle blancuras en serranas, y gente de playa curtidas al sol
y al agua'.[102]

Next, if we grant that pallor is an acceptable attribute, is it too much of an
exaggeration to describe it as whiteness? This is once again an area in which dead
trope is a factor. So-called 'white' skin is typically pale rather than white, and 'black'
skin dark rather than black. However, when in poetry the figurative whiteness of
skin is compared with something which is literally rather than figuratively white, as
in this example of Góngora's, then the situation becomes more complicated, and we
move potentially into the field of wit. The poet's overstatement here is elegantly and
subtly handled. There is wit in the correspondence between the milk and the hands
that produced it, and there is irony in the fact that he singles out the veins
specifically as notably white when arguably their blood supply is the thing most
calculated to detract from the purity of the whiteness of the hand. But having
heightened his description in this fashion, Góngora then qualifies it with the word
'apenas', which indicates that the colour is not indistinguishable from milk.

A more extreme case of hyperbole on which, for once, Jáuregui fails to comment,
is contained in the nuptial songs, where the bride is described as a

> virgen tan bella, que hacer podría
> tórrida la Noruega con dos soles,
> y blanca la Etiopia con dos manos. (I, 783-5)

In a case such as this, literary and even social conventions affect the reader's response
in a similar way to that in which linguistic convention does in the case of lexicalised
trope. The recognition that Góngora's images relate to a long Petrarchan tradition
tends to diminish our sense of the extremity of his exaggeration. As the centuries
progress, a kind of inflation in poetic imagery sets in. The comparison between
bright eyes and stars becomes too hackneyed to be usable. The more radiant sun then
becomes the term of comparison, used ingeniously in the ballad of *Angélica y
Medoro*, and in the *Polifemo*. In the lines quoted above from the *Soledades* Góngora
turns the screw further still and draws attention to the sun as a source of heat rather
than of brightness, as if eyes which are only metaphorically suns could outperform
the real sun in its natural effects. But Góngora's statement is rescued from absurdity
if we read 'tórrida' as a metaphor describing the emotional effects which the beauty of
the bride's eyes might have, arousing the passions of the Norwegians. In the same
way the 'whitening' of Ethiopia, a land of black people, does not have to be seen as a
preposterous statement of an impossible optical effect, but is also susceptible to the
more abstract interpretation that in an Ethiopian context the bride's hands might be
the focus of attention, making people completely oblivious of all others.

The social convention mentioned above which again affects our view of the
acceptability of these hyperboles is our awareness that at formal occasions such as

---

[102]   *La batalla en torno a Góngora*, ed. A. Martínez Arancón, p.27

weddings, with their speeches or songs of praise, the special importance of the event merits a degree of emotional overstatement.

Jáuregui ends his series of complaints about Góngora's use of hyperbole by singling out examples of the description of the stunned reactions firstly of the wanderer to a hilltop view, and secondly of the spectators to the feats of the athletes in conceits whose admirable features have been examined earlier in this book. The first of these, 'muda, la admiración habla callando' with its elegant use of trope to express dumbstruck wonder is arguably not a case of exaggeration at all, save insofar as tropes other than hyperbole in general are to be taken with a pinch of salt. Jáuregui's point is partly that the object of admiration is not worthy of such an extreme reaction. Góngora, with his enthusiasm for the beauties of nature, no doubt felt that it was. Similarly the sub-text of Jáuregui's dismissive comments about the conceits concerning the athletics match is that young peasants in particular, and perhaps sport in general, are not worth the 'hype'. In the case of the reaction to the long-jump, 'la admiración, vestida un marmol frío, /apenas arquear las cejas pudo', it is worth noting again the presence of the moderating 'apenas'. As for the details of the jumper's performance, however impressive or credible its distance of three darts' lengths may or may not be, Góngora makes the point that the young man's fellow competitors find it a daunting target to beat. However, there is no doubting that Jáuregui's final example of description of the spectator's reaction to the runners 'siguiendo el más lento, cojea el pensamiento', at which he expresses such irritation, is a full-blown hyperbole. But the wit of its structure could legitimately be regarded as so enjoyable as to justify the liberty taken. The brain metaphorically limps behind the sprinters as it tries to take in what it has seen, and the expected hierarchy of speed between thought and action is ironically reversed.

The above examples from Góngora illustrate some of the complexities in making judgments about whether a poet has gone too far. One conclusion to be drawn is that the issue as to whether decorum has been violated by the excessive importance given to a lowly object need not relate to the quality of the wit as such but to one's judgment as to the worth of the subject matter. The converse question as to whether wit should be seen as diminishing noble themes will be considered later in this chapter in relation to verbal wit.

A further conclusion from our considerations is that as a trope, hyperbole shares with other tropes the fact that when understood literally it will seem to some degree nonsensical or excessive. That is precisely what enables us to recognize it as a trope. However, the reader faced with an apparent excess of this kind may for a variety of reasons fail to a greater or lesser degree to 'tone down' the expression until it makes rational sense. In some such cases the reader's unawareness of literary tradition such as Petrarchan conventions, for example, may be the cause. In others, the reader's motives may be suspect, as in the case of Jáuregui who was obviously more interested in parading what could be seen as his own unreasonableness as an unreasonableness on the part of the author. A similar bad faith can be seen in some deconstructionist readings of literature which have a vested interest in making literature seem absurd.

I now turn to criticisms made of conceits which err on the side of deficiency rather than of excess. Joseph Addison's analysis of the difference between true, false and mixed wit provides a convenient starting point for the discussion. The set of six daily articles which he produced in the *Spectator* in 1711 concentrate most of their energy into a critique of what he sees as false wit.[103] The basic principle for him is that false wit involves relationships between words, and true wit relationships between ideas, with mixed wit being a hybrid combining the two, and being 'more or less perfect as the resemblance lies in the ideas or in the words.'

Before considering Addison's treatment of the pun as an example of false wit, it is interesting to analyse other rarer breeds which raise the question of what the minimum requirements for wit are. Probably many people would doubt with Addison whether the printing of a poem about a butterfly in the shape of a butterfly's wing constitutes true wit. Not that the correspondence in such a case is between words as Addison suggests. Rather it is between the physical appearance of the poem and the physical appearance of the object it describes. We may see the end result as amusing or charming, but probably not as especially clever. The same may be said of acrostic poems, which again rely on typographical manipulation, and again are relatively easily contrived. And yet effects of some subtlety can be achieved by the way words are distributed in a poem. For example, Góngora's sonnet 'Oh claro honor del líquido elemento' (Millé 220) is much enhanced by the placing of words in the following lines:

Pues la por quien helar y arder me siento
mientras en tí se mira amor retrata
de su rostro la nieve y escarlata

The poet achieves here a transformation of two commonplaces images, the first of the lover going all hot and cold, the second of the girl's complexion combining snowy whiteness and red. By placing *helar* and *nieve* in parallel positions in their respective lines he is able to suggest, without openly stating it, a causal connection between the snow and the lover's feeling cold, and lead us to make a further connection between the 'warm' colour scarlet and 'arder'. There is no lack of sharpness in this conceit which relies ultimately on the positioning of words as a subtle means of attracting our attention to a relationship between two conventional pairs of contrasted words.

Some kinds of artistic manœuvres, unlike acrostics, place extraordinary demands on the writer's inventiveness. Addison mentions the Greek poem with each canto named after a different letter of the Greek alphabet and contrived so that each canto avoided the use of the letter of the alphabet after which it was named. The noble art is revived in the twentieth century by Georges Perec's remarkable novel, *La*

---

[103]   See *The Spectator* (London, 1822), 6 vols, Vol 1, pp. 229-241.

disparition, in which the disappearance in question is that of the vowel 'e', the most common letter of the alphabet, which is completely absent from his text.[104] The scheme is spoiled only by the 'e's which pepper Perec's own name. Nobody doubts that this is a tour de force, and that it is subtly done. But is it wit? Perhaps it is difficult to reconcile with definitions of wit based on the idea of relationships. But at times Perec does, I believe, achieve a kind of correspondence where he indulges in parody, re-writing some well-known poems without the offending 'e', thereby inviting us to compare the original with his version. Particularly sharp is his choice of Mallarmé's poem about vowels as one of these parodied poems. This example shows once again that the manipulation of what we would probably think of as external features of a literary work can be handled with subtlety and are capable of being a medium for striking conceits.

The case of the missing vowel can be thought of as an extreme instance of the artist accepting self-imposed constraints and where possible making a virtue out of these by overcoming them in a way which looks wholly convincing. The use of such a tightly disciplined form as the sonnet is a case in point. We might also apply it to the use of a particularly challenging rhyming scheme. Addison includes 'double rhymes' in his list of examples of false wit, and we could no doubt add to it other instances of difficult rhymes, where the language has a limited number of possibilities on offer. Quevedo's disgusting encapsulation of the whole of human life in his sonnet 'La vida empieza en lágrimas y caca' with its difficult and suitably cacaphonic rhymes in *-aca -eca* and *-uca* might serve as an example. Or there is Góngora's comic poem 'Despuntado he mil agujas' (Millé, 42), which though masquerading as a *romance* in fact uses rhyme rather than assonance at the end of the even numbered lines, and displays no less than fifty rhymes in *-ote*. A similar display of virtuosity is found in his *romance* 'Tendiendo sus blancos paños' (Millé, 35), which achieves a similar half-century of rhymes in *-ete*.

All these cases of the manipulation of what can be thought of as external features of the text are on the margins of wit. But whether we should concur with Addison in placing verbal wit in the same category is another matter. Admittedly he was not alone in despising word play, and still today the pun is popularly regarded as 'the lowest form of wit'. We need to analyse the reasons for this low regard, and to see how far practice corresponds to theory.

The fact that Addison sees punning as no different in principle from the exploitation of typographical features in a poem suggests that he sees it as based primarily on the physical characteristic of similarity of sound. Such a view pays scant regard to the linguistic function of the words used, and its inadequacy is exposed straight away when we consider the typical pun in which a single word or expression is simultaneously used in different senses. In such a case sound patterns play no part.

---

[104]   (Paris, *Les Lettres Nouvelles*, Editions Denoël, 1969), 319 pp.

Some comments made by Peregrini in *Delle acutezze* seem to indicate that the downgrading of verbal wit may be the result of a crude and inadequate philosophy of language which thinks basically in terms of nouns and their referents. On the one hand there are words, seen as insubstantial, 'mere' words, on the other hand, things, which have a more important status. Verbal wit, seen in this light, relates words merely to other words instead of to things. But if we abandon this very limiting and blinkered account of language it becomes apparent that there is in reality no difficulty in analysing verbal wit in terms of a *correspondencia* if we see it as relating different uses of language. It is a case of revealing patterns in our linguistic behaviour which are in principle no less substantial, worthy or interesting than patterns to be found in other phenomena.

Sarbiewski is another theorist who downgrades verbal wit.   The distinction between the two very similar terms *acutum* and *argutum* which he makes towards the end of his treatise on wit is made when he acknowledges that one could object to his theory that not all types of wit conform to his definition of the conceit as consisting in a *discordia concors*. Conceding this point, he says that these deviant forms of wit are not true examples of the *acutum*, that we should refer in such cases to the *argutum*, and that most instances of this lesser kind of wit are based on word play. This certainly seems to be the Achilles' heel of his theory.   The device of marginalizing cases which do not fit one's own definition looks suspect, and Sarbiewski can hardly been said to have demonstrated why conceits which lack a discordant element should be regarded as inferior. Moreover, in the case of verbal wit, the tension between different uses of the same word could be analysed just as easily in terms of a *discordia concors* as many examples of non-verbal wit.

A further general reason for the generally low reputation of verbal wit is the assumption that it invariably lowers the tone and is incompatible with true seriousness. Jáuregui, who is alert to the puns in Góngora's *Soledades* describes them as burlesque:

> Unos pensamientos o conceptos burlescos gasta Vm. en esta obra y en todas las suyas, indignísimas de Poesía ilustre y merecedores de grande reprehensión, aunque a Vm. quizá le parescan galantes.

He adds a little later, "generalmente son raterísimos todos los juegos del vocablo".

Such a negative attitude towards verbal wit is not shared by Gracián, who initially toys with the idea of a basic classification of conceits which distinguishes between the conceptual conceit, and the verbal conceit

> que consiste más en la palabra; de tal modo que se aquélla se quita, no queda alma, ni se pueden éstas traducir a otra lengua.

Although he goes on to adopt a different taxonomy he does include four chapters devoted to verbal conceits, the 'agudeza nominal', which exploits the significance to be found in names, the 'agudeza por paranomasia, retruécano y jugar del vocablo', which exploits the juxtaposition of words with a similar but not identical form, 'los ingeniosos equívocos' which exploit multiple meanings, and 'los conceptos por acomodación de verso antiguo, de algún texto o autoridad' which are allusive conceits. Only the third of these, equivocation, is singled out as lacking in seriousness:

> Son poco graves los conceptos por equívoco, y así más aptos para sátiras
> y cosas burlescas que para lo serio y prudente'.

I shall discuss the rationale behind regarding equivocation as frivolous a little later. But first it is worth noting the soundness of regarding the other types of conceit as compatible with seriousness.

Firstly, take the play on names, which is often exploited by Góngora in his poetry. Sometimes the technique is used in jest in his satirical and burlesque poetry, as for example in his sonnet mocking the court at Valladolid

> Todo sois Condes, no sin nuestro daño,
> Dígalo el Andaluz que en un infierno
> debajo de una tabla escrita posa.
> No encuentra al de Buendía en todo el año,
> · al de Chinchón si ahora, y el invierno,
> al de Niebla, al de Nieve, al de Lodosa.

Ostensibly the poet is referring to the presence or absence of particular named Counts at court, but the context makes it clear that he is jocularly commenting on the presence or absence of conditions which the various names allude to if we give them meaning instead of treating them merely as tags with which to identify individuals. The virtuoso quality of this conceit derives from the number of pertinent examples given.

The technique in itself, however, is not what produces the comic effect, as can be seen by considering examples where the tone is very different. For example, the name Conde de Niebla again appears in the dedication to Góngora's *Polifemo*. The words which figuratively read ('ahora que de luz tu Niebla doras') refer to the honour which the Count's presence bestows upon his local community form a pleasing pattern when 'niebla' is read as a noun rather than a name, and 'dorar' is read literally, meaning 'to gild', evoking a picture of sunlight gilding the fog. Another poem in which the name this time of the Marques de Flores is subtly used is one in which Góngora having been laid low by an illness writes a poem to the Marquis on the transience of life. The wit comes from the series of images derived from the kingdom of flowers, emblems of the brevity of life, a series which corresponds to the meaning attributable to the Marquis's name. At the same time, and ironically, Góngora could be taken to be addressing a warning to the flowers rather than the Marquis. His illness sends a message to the flowers, when traditionally it is the brief life of flowers which is taken by the moralists as sending a message to man. Finally, we can find another perfectly serious example of play on a name in the sonnet addressed to Cristóbal de Mora (Millé, 256), which draws an extended and ingenious analogy between the Marquis and a mulberry tree, on the basis of the significance of his name. A tree which if the patronage Góngora aspires to is forthcoming will sustain the poet as metaphorical silkworm spinning verses and protect him as a metaphorical bird singing his praises.

In between the two extremes of the comic and the serious we have examples which seem elusively to span both. Góngora's half-comic half-serious poem dedicated to St Teresa of Avila (Millé 69) is a case in point. It is a poem of genuine admiration rather than a satire, yet with a light, witty touch. The poet draws attention to a relationship between the meaning of the saint's family name and the name of the learned theologian, 'El Tostado'. She may not have equalled him in scholarship, states Góngora, but at least their names were matched.

The 'agudeza nominal', then, though exploitable for comic purposes, is not inherently comic. One could also argue, moreover, that it is indistinguishable in principle from equivocation since it exploits the ambiguity of a word, and therefore there may be nothing inherently comic in equivocation.

With Gracián's next example of verbal wit, paronomasia, again there is no shortage of examples to suggest that there is nothing comic about it in principle. At its simplest, however, it may not be perceived as wit at all, and since the correspondence established by it is basically that of sound, it fits well enough Addison's concept of false wit. One question that it gives rise to is how far it differs in principle from rhyme, which also displays words similar in sound but different in meaning, but which is not usually thought of as embodying wit. It is not easy to work out exactly why we should see Góngora's invocation to Cupid as the 'vendado que me has vendido' as sharper than any rhyme taken at random from his poetry such as 'En tenebrosa noche con pie incierto,/La confusión pisando del desierto.' Another form of word-play typical in late fifteenth-century poetry which is not noted for its wit, is polyptoton, alias *annominatio*, where the poet may string together a whole series of words based on the same linguistic root. In this latter case perhaps it is simply that the end-product is simply too ponderously obvious, and lacks all subtlety.

Two examples of paronomasia in Góngora will suffice as examples which are integrated into genuine conceits and which, I would claim, offer no threat to the decorum. The first is sneered at by Jáuregui as an example of unworthy word-play. It is set within a description of a dead-heat between three runners hastening to reach and cling to a trio of elms ('hercúleos troncos' because the elm is associated with Hercules in classical myth).

> Arbitro Alcides en sus ramas, dudo
> que el caso decidiera,
> bien que su menor hoja un ojo fuera
> del lince más agudo (I, 1061-4)

Firstly the wit of this passage does not rely on primarily on the 'hoja' 'ojo' word-play. Góngora amplifies the simultaneity of the runners by illustrating how it would have defeated the very highest standards of observation, by firstly envisaging the closest vantage-point possible right at the very finishing posts, and secondly imagining the God Hercules himself as the observer situated in the very trees dedicated to him, and finally by picturing each tree as a metamorphosed God whose very leaves are the sharpest of eyes. The approximate correspondence between the shape of leaves and eyes adds sharpness to the passage, and a final aesthetic touch is added by the correspondence of the sounds of the words.

My second illustration comes from a panegyric poem on the occasion of a voyage undertaken by The Marquis of Ayamonte (Millé 283). The ships ('naves') are metaphorically described as clouds ('nubes') which in turn are metaphorically referred to as chariots of a sun. Here the word play offers but one ingredient in a complex series of correspondences. Firstly the physical similarity between full sails and clouds provides the basis of the first metaphor, the next image of the chariot works in relation to the boat in that both carry radiant passengers, although in the case of the boat the radiance is metaphorical. What adds sharpness to the passage is the connection between clouds and chariots, in that clouds obscure the sun, which offers an ingenious explanation of why at a distance we would not see this particular 'sun'. Rather than seeing this as an example of *discordia concors* we might see Góngora's ingenuity as working to dissolve an element of tension which is present in the metaphor of the sun and raise the degree of connectedness between the terms of the correspondence.

Gracián borrows the 'naves-nubes' word-play in his *Criticón* where the innocent Andrenio seeing for the first time in his life ships on the horizon, describes them as clouds. Critilo corrects him, saying that they are but ships, although in a sense they are indeed clouds raining gold on Spain. Again the writer offers us a further ingenious justification for the cloud metaphor apart from that of physical resemblance. And in both Góngora's and Gracián's conceits the word-play can hardly be said to lower the tone.

The type of conceit classified by Gracián as consisting in the adaptation of a citation from some text or other, although identified as a case of verbal wit can be seen as part of a wider phenomenon of allusive wit, which sometimes relies on a precise form of words, and sometimes relies merely on our perception of a parallel situation between the new text and the text or story alluded to. For example, we find a comic adaptation of Matthew 5,5, from Christ's Sermon on the Mount, "Beati qui persectuionem patiuntur propter iustitiam", rendered in Spanish as 'los que padecen persecuciones por justicia', referring in its new context to the torture to extract a confession undergone by Lazarillo's thief of a father at the hands of the legal authorities. The passages turns on the equivocal use of 'por', which in the Biblical context means 'for the sake of', and in the case of Lazarillo's father obviously means 'at the hands of'. In Góngora, two puns in the *Soledades* mocked by Jáuregui are also based on Biblical allusion. The first describes goat's meat served up at a meal as coming from a he-goat 'que con su muerte redimió tantas vides' (I, 160). The connection of death and redemption inevitably conjures up thoughts of Christ's death of whom it could be said that he redeemed many lives 'tantas vidas', whereas in the case of the goat it is the vines ('vides') which he used to nibble which are rescued by his death. The ironic parallel is completed by the implicit paronomasia. The second example again depends on our recognition of a form of words which though not a quotation as such might have been appropriate for describing another Biblical situation. At the wedding feast in the first *Soledad* stomachs of the drinking revellers would not have been settled but for the eating of olives: 'si la sabrosa oliva no serenara el bacanal diluvio' (I, 881-2), cleverly translated by Cunningham thus:

... but for the aid
the savoury olive brought,
Which once had calmed a greater flood than these[105]

thereby proving that the test for verbal wit of untranslatability proposed by Addison and before him Gracián is unreliable. The metaphorical flood of the drinking bout parallels that faced by Noah's arc, whose conclusion was also signalled by the olive, though on that occasion the olive leaf brought back by the dove.

If decorum is threatened here, the indirectness of allusion, and in the case of the description of the goat the subtlety of implied paronomasia mitigates the effect. But it is the respect owed to the Bible as a text which provides the potential for a sense of burlesque rather than the verbal parallels created. One can demonstrate the point by noting Góngora's use of a more lowly text, *Lazarillo de Tormes*, in which the lovesick Góngora describes himself as a second Lazarillo and expresses the hope that he too will be able to take revenge on 'el ciego', the blind one, which in his case is clearly Cupid. The touch is light, but wholly in keeping with the poem in which it appears, and the wit is verbal in that it relies on an equivocal reading of 'ciego' rather than being strictly speaking verbally reliant on a quotation.

At the same time, Góngora shows how in his burlesque poetry, where decorum is deliberately breached, the comic effect of the allusive conceit in no way leaves us with a sense that his inventiveness is in any way inferior to that of his more serious poems. For example, the *romance* 'Aunque entiendo poco griego', telling the story of Hero and Leander (Millé, 64), mocks Leander's inadequacy as a serenader by describing the effect of his nocturnal singing with allusions to the rather more desirable results achieved by Orpheus and Amphion.

Orfeo tan desgraciado
que nunca enfrenó las aguas
que convocó el dulce canto
puesto que ya de Anfión
imitando algunos pasos,
llamó a sí más piedras
que tuvo el muro tebano.

---

105   Gibert F. Cunningham, *The Solitudes of Luis de Góngora y Argote*, (Alva, 1964), line 880.

Leander's failure to emulate Orpheus whose song stopped rivers in their course ('nunca enfrenó las aguas') involves an ironic understatement: not only did he fail to stop the flow, but, reading between the lines, we understand that he actually attracted the slops poured on him from the balconies of those whose ears were offended by his efforts, which in turn leads us to appreciate the irony of the adjective 'dulce' used to describe his song. On the other hand, he outdoes Amphion in the number of stones he attracts, the irony this time residing in the reality underlying the euphemistic verb which fails to spell out that the stones were clearly aimed at him by a hostile audience. The brilliance of the wit here lies not merely in the individual examples but also in the agreeable correspondence derived from their pairing. The effect is similar to that of the double reference to the legend of Narcissus in the first *Soledad*, where the tone is obviously not comic, in which in the line 'ecos solicitar, desdeñar fuentes' (I, 116) the modern Narcissus is described metaphorically as seeking out echoes, unlike the classical Narcissus who literally spurned the nymph Echo, and as metaphorically shunning springs, again unlike the legendary Narcissus who could not tear himself away from the stream in which he saw his own reflection.

Whether or not it makes sense to categorize such allusive conceits as instances of verbal wit, they demonstrate that by its very indirectness allusion is subtler than direct statement, and particularly where compound examples are integrated into a particular context the sense of pleasing correspondence is strong.

What of the equivocal use of words as a source of wit? How justified is its low reputation? Certainly there are examples of Golden-Age conceits of dubious quality based on double meanings. One of the disconcerting features of Gracián's treatise on wit is the relatively unimpressive quality of many of his examples. It is not simply that in quoting Góngora he ignores many of his finest conceits in favour of others less worthy, but that at times his taste seems suspect. For instance, he chooses as his illustration of *agudeza pura*, a conceit of Alonso Girón de Rebolledo, whom he describes as an 'agudísimo poeta', from a poem on Christ's Passion, which says of the cock crowing when Peter denied Christ:

> No había de cantar el gallo
> viendo tan grande gallina?

This example is discussed with due seriousness by more than one British critic without any hint of the bewilderment expressed by Antonio Carreira at seeing what to most modern eyes surely looks like a cheap pun in the context of a poem which is apparently not setting out to offer a burlesque degradation of its sombre subject matter.[106] Yet the lapse in decorum is arguably attributable largely to the low register of *gallina* rather than to the fact that it is used equivocally. This can be demonstrated by finding an example of punning in a sombre context where the register of the words is higher. For an example of a deadly serious pun we could do worse than turn to Shakespeare, whose heroes are accused by Addison of

---

106   Luis de Góngora, *Antología poética*, ed. A. Carreira, (Madrid, Castalia, 1989), p. 53

inappropriately 'quibbling for dozens of lines at a time'. Yet I suspect that nobody is likely to see anything irritating or comic in Othello's words as he plans the killing of Desdemona "Put out the light, then put out the light". Word play here enhances rather than diminishes the tragedy with its irony, and the vocabulary used is entirely appropriate to the context. Ruth Wallerstein illustrates with other lines from Hamlet a tradition of an implied tragedy of tone in pun and wordplay in Shakespeare and the Metaphysical poets, emphasising its intellectual nature.[107]

An analogous case to that of Girón de Rebolledo is discussed by R. O. Jones, who draws attention to the tastelessness of some of Alonso de Ledesma's conceits in his *Conceptos espirituales*, where the brutal martyrdom of the saints is treated with what might seem like flippancy. He cites, *inter alia,* the lines on Saint Agueda with her breasts mutilated:

Ya que no iguala la esposa
al dulce esposo que espera,
a lo menos no es pechera.

The key pun here is 'pechera' which has the double meaning 'busty' or 'a commoner'. Jones, noting Ledesma's distastefully barbarous imagination, and his 'cheerful brutality' comments: "the *kind* of imagination he possessed --drawing all manner of things together in his analogies — is the kind that underlies the best writing of the period. What we can legitimately object to is the *quality* of his imagination, at once coarse and shallow." [*A Literary History of Spain. The Golden Age: Prose and Poetry* (London, Benn, 1974), p. 147]

The grotesque effect of these lines is the result of a combination of factors. Firstly, at the physical level, there is the callousness of the understatement of 'no pechera' to describe the victim of a savage mastectomy. Secondly, on the alternative reading of 'no pechera' there is the indecorous irrelevance of social considerations in considering the appropriateness of God receiving a particular soul. Spiritually speaking, the martyr's virtue and sanctity are nobler and more relevant factors in which the poet shows no interest.

Another conceit of Ledesma's which parallels one of Góngora's illustrates further the independence of the type of wit on the one hand and the tastefulness or otherwise of the end result on the other. Describing another martyr, St Stephen, facing death by stoning, Ledesma describes him as his own lapidary, a display of stones shaped by his own blood. This is a pun only to the extent that 'piedra' is ambiguous, meaning both an ordinary stone and a gem. The additional correspondence which is important here is the legendary belief that noble blood was capable of softening the hardest of gem-stones. The same idea is exploited to quite different effect by Góngora in his *Romance de Angélica y Medoro* (Millé 48) where the oriental princess, formerly

---

107 *Studies in Seventeenth-Century Poetic* (Madison-Milwaukee, University of Wisconsin Press, 1965), p.169 ff.

unresponsive to men, falls in love with the wounded Medoro, who has lost much blood. Here love is described as lurking between the roses (of Medoro's cheeks)

> Porque labren sus arpones
> el diamante del Catay
> con aquella sangre noble

In this context it is the word 'diamond' which has the double meaning: just as a real diamond might be softened by blood, so the metaphorical diamond, the princess, is metaphorically softened by the sight of Medoro's blood. In Góngora's case the lyrical tone of the poem is maintained, and the princess is not lowered in our eyes by the metaphor of the diamond. In Ledesma's case the heartless idea of the saint's body in its agony being regarded in a quite detached way as a kind of work of art rather than a suffering being reveals seriously bad taste. The difference resides in the context and not the intellectual structure of the conceit.

One more example of linguistic wit which is by no means out of place is to be found in Fray Luis de León's famous poem *Vida retirada*.[108] In what is described by L. J. Woodward as a 'profound pun', the poet questions the value of the pursuit of fame 'si en busca de este viento ando desalentado'. Where the literal sense of 'desalentado' — 'breathless' — relates ironically to the metaphor 'viento' used to describe fame, suggesting the useless expenditure of air in pursuit of what itself is figuratively speaking no more than empty air.

No doubt the general bias against verbal wit is fuelled by our awareness that puns are often used jocularly and form the basis of many jokes. Again the use of the term 'play' to refer to punning encourages us to take it lightly. But we should beware of begging the question in accepting such a term. In a sense all art is play, but that does not mean that none of it is to be taken seriously.

It seems, then, that punning is not in itself bound to produce levity, and that conceits with a very similar logical structure may show greater or lesser degrees of decorousness. If we now take the argument a stage further it is possible to see how distinctions of quality can be made within the comic genre. A light hearted conceit is not by that token a manifestation of inferior wit. Some of Góngora's most memorable and impressive conceits are to be found in his lighter works.

The criterion I shall use, already discussed in part earlier in this chapter, is that of the degree of conectedness between the terms of the conceit. The more ways the elements in the conceit are connected, or the greater the number of elements brought together, and the perfection with which they fit together then the more impressive the conceit will seem.

At the bottom end of the scale are those conceits which are comic precisely because of the poor quality of the match. Into this category fall those puns which involve double meanings, only one of which really fits the situation described by the

---

108   L.J. Woodward, '*La vida retirada* of Fray Luis de León', *Bulletin of Hispanic Studies*, 31 (1954), pp. 17-26

poet, and the other of which is nonsense. Where the author seems to force on the reader the more nonsensical of the two readings the result is simply silly. A case in point is Doña Alda's comment in Góngora's *romance* 'Diez años vivió Belerma' (Millé 9),

> De todos los doce Pares
> y sus nones abrenuncio.

Here the word 'nones', 'odd numbers', only fits its companion word 'pares' when it is read to mean 'even numbers', but in this context the twelve 'pares' can only sensibly be read to mean the knights of the round table, alias the twelve peers. Again the *romance* addressed to the castle of San Cervantes (Millé 34) contains the following silly joke:

> Lampiño debes de ser,
> castillo, si no estoy ciego,
> pues siendo de tantos años
> sin barbacana te veo.

The castle is described as lacking facial hair ('lampiño') on the grounds that it has no 'barbacana', a word which in its printed form means 'barbican', but which sounds the same as the two words 'barba cana', 'white beard'. It is perhaps worth noting the marginally improved fit in this example since clearly not only is no barbican visible, but nor is any white beard. But then, one would not expect to see a white beard on a castle, hence the silliness of the sentence.

In similar vein is Góngora's description of an impoverished suitor:

> camafeo de la moza
> ser el necio pretendía
> y al la verdad era feo
> aunque cama no tenía.

However, here the splitting of the word results in a slightly sharper logic. It is as if the suitor's aspiration to be the girl's favourite (her 'cameo' in the sense that she is likely to carry a cameo portrait of her beloved) could be achieved in stages by the acquisition of features referred to by the first and second half of the relevant word. The easier half has been achieved by the lad's natural ugliness, but his poverty, which means he has no bed to sleep in, denies him the acquisition of the remaining feature.

Where the alternative readings of a pun both fit the context then the effect is no longer inherently comic. For example, although Jáuregui condemned as burlesque Góngora's description in the *Soledades* of the woodland canopy of trees as 'bóvedas de sombras, /pintadas siempre al fresco' (I, 612-3) the register of the vocabulary does not lower the tone, and the phrase 'al fresco' fits both the metaphorical reading of painted vaults, and the literal reading of shady tree-tops.

Sometimes extra links are provided in verbal conceits by being part of a coherent series. Compare, for example, the following:

> En tanto que mis vacas
> sin oillos, condenan

> en frutos los madroños
> desta fragosa sierra (Millé 47)

and:

> Moral que los hospedó
> y fue condenado al punto,
> si de el Tigris no en raíces
> de los amantes en fructos. (Millé 74, lines 25-7)

In the first passage Góngora puns on the legal phrase 'condenar en frutos' which normally refers to the confiscation of income from capital as opposed to 'condenar en raíces' which is the confiscation of capital. The cows confiscate the income/fruits of the wild strawberry plants 'sin oillos' — without giving them a hearing in court. It is the presence of this last phrase which makes the conceit silly. In the second passage this element is absent, and in addition Góngora manages to work in the twin phrase 'condenado en raíces'. If the river does not flood the roots of the tree, then the blood of the dead lovers will contaminate the fruits of the mulberry, turning them red. In other words there is a higher level of correspondence in the second example, although what reduces its sense of remarkableness is the fact that the twin legal expressions obviously originally derive from a botanical metaphor, and so the possibility of reapplying them to a botanical context was always there.

A far more brilliant sequence of the paired pun because it does not come ready made is that used to describe in burlesque fashion the death of two other lovers, Hero and Leander. Hero's epitaph reads:

> El Amor como dos huevos
> quebrantó nuestras saludes:
> él fue pasado por agua,
> yo estrellado mi fin tuve. (Millé 27)

Here the paired phrases 'pasado por agua' and 'estrellado' both apply to methods of cooking eggs — boiling and frying. At the same time both apply to the cause of death of the two lovers, Leander drowning, and Hero smashed to death when she jumps from the tower. The perfect double pun is further enhanced by yet another pun 'como dos huevos' which is a standard expression, equivalent to the English 'as like as two peas in a pod', which refers to remarkable similarity, using eggs as the standard for indistinguishability. As alike as two eggs, the two lovers die in ways which whose description could also refer to the cooking of two eggs.

The irreverence in this passage derives not from the fact that there is verbal play here, but to the reduction of the death of two human beings to the language of the kitchen. Where there is no disparity between the linguistic register and the subject matter then a pun need offer no threat to the tone. See for example, the pun on 'cama de viento' in Góngora's *Polifemo* (line 215), which does not disrupt the lyricism of the sensual scene described.

A complex sequence of ideas which reveals Góngora's brilliant word-play at its best is to be found in his *Firmezas de Isabela,* a play much admired by Gracián for its wit. In his first entry, the comic servant Tadeo comments amusingly on his own inability to keep a secret:

> pues con propiedad no poca
> imito a la comadreja
> que se empreña por la oreja
> para parir por la boca.
>
> Y de la arte que embaraza
> doblón al que ha de gastalle,
> que sale luego a trocalle
> en menudos a la plaza;
>
> tal yo inclinado, y sujeto
> a lo que el Cielo le plugo,
> pregonero, y aun verdugo,
> hago cuartos un secreto. (lines 166-177)

First the popular legend of the weasel is applied with a perfect match this time with 'empreñar' and 'parir' being understood metaphorically to the action of a gossip repeating what he has heard, and magnifying the story in re-telling it. Then follows the quite different but no less sharp comparison between the gossip and one who cannot wait to change into coins of smaller denomination a coin of embarassingly high value. The match here is in the process of splitting which is applicable to the repetition of the same story to a large number of people, and the idea of going into the public square to achieve this where one would find plenty of company. The final twist to the sequence comes in pairing of *pregonero* and *verdugo*, officials whose duties brought them together when criminals were publicly punished and humiliated, but whose functions logically fit the role of the gossip who, like a town crier, announces secrets for all to hear, and like an executioner, in so doing kills those secrets off. Finally there is the correspondence provided by the pun 'hacer cuartos' which relates both to an executioner quartering his victims, and to the person changing a dubloon into four smaller coins. The pun provides the unexpected link between the person seeking change and the executioner.

The pleasure to be enjoyed in this complex sequence offering wit of the highest quality is similar to that in Góngora's famous description of Galatea's complexion and her pearl earring in his *Polifemo* (lines 105-112). The passage exploits in a fresh metaphorically way traditionally paired terms 'empreñar' and 'parir', 'pregonero' and 'verdugo', and finishes with a double metaphor in the equivocal reading of 'hacer cuartos' which refers both to multiplication and to destruction. What is pleasing is the way these multiple elements all function so well together, with the final pun putting the icing on the cake. There is no *discordia concors* here. Instead perfect harmony reigns.

Another brilliant sequence drawn from the world of music and capped by a pun can be found in the burlesque *romance,* 'Cuando la rosada Aurora' (Millé 54) where a doctor's mule, having covered the ground in droppings 'en sólo un abrir de ojo', referred to in the text metaphorically as gold dubloons, sees his master leaping about in his efforts to extricate himself from the mess, thinks he is dancing, and provides some 'music' for the dance:

El macho piensa que baila,
y porque no falte son,
ya que ha engomado las cerdas,
su rabelillo tocó.
Dióle viento, y fue organillo.

Having 'rosined his bow' ('engomado las cerdas'), the horsehair being sticky in this case through contact with the filth, he plays his rebec which becomes converted by the application of wind rather than just hair into a chamber organ as the creature breaks wind. The arranged doctor plucks a 'baton' from a nearby tree to 'give him the beat'. But the animal, anxious to avoid a beating, performs a 'four part fugue' ('fuga a cuatro pies'), the four parts being the four feet ('pies') with which he flees.

Pues a un árbol de aquel prado
pidió apriesa un varejón,
para llevalle el compás;
mas el macho no aguardó.
Hizo fuga a cuatro pies.

On the basis of all the examples given in this chapter we are now in a position to draw some conclusions about the factors determining the quality of conceits and reassess the views of the various theorists. In doing so, we should take care to not to confuse the issue of the quality of wit with that of decorum.

Firstly, as far as the quality of wit is concerned, it makes sense to see a hierarchy of conceits starting with those in which there is a minimum of elements minimally connected and eventually moving on to those in which there may be large number of elements all perfectly matched. At the bottom of the scale some of Addison's examples of false wit, such as paronomasia, may show us a minimal wit based on a simple correspondence of the sounds of different words. At a more sophisticated level, the exploitation of a double meaning for a single expression opens up the potential for a much more impressive correspondence between elements, which makes Addison's lumping together of all types of verbal wit as inferior unsatisfactory. True there may be an obvious falseness in the kind of pun in which one of two readings is nonsensical and the mismatch is comically exploited by the author. But where the competing readings of a pun function harmoniously together the result can be impressive.

As far as decorum is concerned, this is independent of the quality of the wit. Hence, as we have seen, a minimal conceit using paronomasia need offer no threat to the lyrical tone of a poem. Conversely, wit of the highest standard showing an impressive network of connections can be seen at work in a burlesque poem such as Góngora's *romance* on Hero and Leander, where the noble characters are belittled not by the presence of verbal wit, but by the dehumanizing nature of the images used.

As we have also seen, there is nothing inherently comic in punning which is by no means incompatible with tragedy or lyricism.

As for flaws which traditionally might be ascribed to some excess on the part of the writer, these can more convincingly be analysed as cases of deficiency. A conceit that is said to be too far fetched, or too exaggerated can be shown to be a conceit in which the logical correspondences are insufficiently convincing. The low level of connectedness between its elements thus relegates it to a low position in the Jáuregui.

The traditionally low status of verbal wit, as I have suggested, needs revision. Gracián has the independence of mind not to despise it in the way that some other theorists did. Even he sees equivocation as basically comic. But, as we have seen, despite the fact that many jokes use puns, there is nothing inherent in the nature of word play to make it necessarily jocular. Not only is verbal wit compatible with seriousness it is also compatible with the artistic revelation of complex and subtle correspondences and is not limited to conceits of the most trivial kind.

To be fair to Addison, in cases where verbal wit is integrated into a complex sequence he might have been prepared to give it a slightly higher status by characterising it as 'mixed wit', which he calls 'a composition of pun and true wit'. His conception of mixed wit is an interesting one, and despite A.A. Parker's assertion that it has no application to Golden-Age wit, in fact offers a fruitful way of looking at a quite common kind of conceit in the period. Addison's examples of mixed wit show that what he mainly has in mind are cases where tropes are sometimes given a literal meaning. This suggests that kind of interplay between literal and figurative wit examined in an earlier chapter insofar as it exploits the multiple meanings of words can legitimately be seen as a kind of verbal wit. But again, the results can be of great subtlety and legitimately be regarded as high points in the art of the conceit. They may equally result in wit of the silliest kind. In other words, their verbal nature in itself tells us nothing about their decorousness or the level of their quality.

Chapter Eight: Profile of a wit

Having studied the range of techniques used by Góngora through specific examples culled from a variety of poems, it remains for me to attempt a general assessment of the role of wit in the various genres which he practised and its place in his output as a whole.

Although Góngora's wit is not restricted to particular types of poem it falls short of being all pervasive. We need to be on our guard against assuming that certain features of his poetry which may well enhance its ability to impress us ipso facto constitute wit. Comic poetry, poetry which shows a lively imagination, or sententious poetry may well show little or no wit, and may be none the worse for that.

To consider comic poetry first, some of Góngora's more entertaining poems are virtually devoid of conceits. A case in point is the charming *romancillo* 'Hermana Marica' in which a young man eagerly anticipates fiesta time (Millé 4). For all its lightness of touch it shows not a shred of wit. In the field of satire, Góngora was adept at comically revealing the unappetising reality underlying the public mask adopted by many members of society. His *letrilla* with the alternating refrains 'bien puede ser' 'no puede ser' (Millé 95) in its very form follows a sequence of such unmaskings, but it is only in the few instances where there is verbal play that the humour becomes wit, as with the *double entendre* about candles:

> Que por parir mil loquillas
> enciendan mil candelillas
> bien puede ser;
> mas que público o secreto
> no haga algún cirio efeto,
> no puede ser

or the brilliant coining of the word 'pulgatorio' to describe the torment of flea bites afflicting the fashion-conscious young man wearing a fancy collar ('un cuello en paraíso'). The bulk of this poem shows no wit.

Jokes share with wit the reliance on surprise for their effect, but unless that surprise is linked to the perception of a *correspondencia* then there is no conceit. One comic technique frequently exploited by Góngora in which the humour depends on the gap between what we are expecting the poet to say and what he actually says is where vacuous statements produce bathos, as for example where in burlesque vein the love-sick shepherd Galayo is mocked (Millé 10). His hand is described as on the end of his wrist instead of anywhere more informative, and he praises the brow of his beloved not for its snowy-whiteness but for being positioned between the girl's temples, and her teeth not for their pearly qualities, but for being in her mouth. In a case where parody takes the form of the mockery of a specific original poem and the reader's expectations are moulded by the structure of the original there is of course a correspondence between the new poem and the old, but the humour is likely to be too unsubtle to qualify as wit.

Even where bathos is based on a strikingly unexpected comparison the effect will not necessarily be due to a witty correspondence. For example, when Góngora says that the writer of 'Hermana Marica', none other than himself,

> tiene por más suya la lengua latina
> que los alemanes
> la persa o egipcia (Millé 24)[109]

the bathos derives from the fact that we were expecting a standard of excellence to be set by the example instead of what is clearly a standard of ignorance rather than from any feature of the correspondence itself. In the context of satirical poetry such unexpected comparisons, when sharply observed, enhance the poet's mockery but do not necessarily involve wit. A good illustration of it is to be found in the very popular satrical *romance* of his, 'Murmuraban los rocines', where he writes

> habló allí un rocín más largo
> que una noche de diciembre
> para un hombre mal casado (Millé 38)[110]

The source of our enjoyment of this incidental reminder of the plight of the henpecked husband is not, I would claim, a witty correspodence. However, where verbal play is also involved comic comparisons of this kind can tilt over into wit. Thus when in the same poem a horse complains that his master

> déjame as la pared
> pegado como gargajo

the surprise stems partly from the double sense of 'pegado' which mixes figurative and literal senses of the word.

The same is true of the comment of one horse that his master keeps changing his bit because 'le pongo en cuatro días/como soneto limado' where the verb 'limar' is used literally in the case of the bit and figuratively in the case of the sonnet.

In some of Góngora's comic poems then, the function of wit is not to provide the whole basis for the humour, but rather to provide an extra spice from time to time. Occasionally conceits may have a more important structural role in a comic poem though. For example, the burlesque *romance* 'Quien es aquel caballero' (Millé 44) includes a punning comparison like those just cited above, where a gallant boasts of 'Sangre más que una morcilla', but in this case this is not an isolated example, as the whole poem is based on a succession of puns. Similarly the comic poem ironically

---

[109]   Poem 24, line 181 in Carreño's edition of the *romances*.
[110]   Poem 38, line 94 in Carreño's edition.

praising the mouldering Castillo de San Cervantes (Millé 34) is essentially structured as a sequence of conceits.

The lively imagination which in the English critical tradition was often equated with wit through the use of the term 'fancy' was no guarantee of wit in Gracián's sense, as one can see from the whimsical but witless little *letrilla* about the swings and roundabouts of fortune, 'Cuando pitos flautas;/cuando flautas pitos' (Millé 97), where we move from the image of the lame goat producing kids, to the haunting one of the young lad swinging from the gibbet for the theft of an egg. Again there is no wit apparent in the sombre visionary sonnet 'Cosas, Celalba mía, he visto extrañas' (Millé 261).

This last example leads us into the question of the role of wit in the sonnet. The existence of the concept of the Petrarcan or sonneteering conceit and our knowledge that a good sonnet requires a rigorous structure and a strong ending leads to expectations that this is a verse form which is particularly likely to manifest wit. But the 'strong lines' which conclude sonnets may owe their strength to their rhetorical pattern or their sententiousness rather than to their wit. Often the conceits in Góngora's sonnets are not reserved for the conclusion. Consider his satire on court life in 'Grandes, más que elefantes' which offers a series of conceits, probably the best of which is the reference to the number of beasts pulling large coaches as matched by the beasts riding inside.[111] The line which rounds it off: 'Esto es la Corte. Buena pro les haga!' rounds the poem off by explicitly voicing the attitude implicit in the previous snide comments, but in terms of wit it does not represent the high point of the poem. One could say the same about Góngora's sombre sonnet on the brevity of life 'Menos solictó veloz saeta' (Millé 374) which has a wonderfully strong ending, helped by the metaphors contained in the verbs and by the balanced rhetorical structure:

> Mal te perdonarán a ti las horas;
> las horas que limando está los días
> los días que royendo están los años

But the sharpest wit of the poem comes earlier with the line 'Cada Sol repetido es un cometa'. Here the use of the metonym 'sun' for 'day' enables the poet to exploit a comparison between the sun and a comet which works at more than one level. The apparently slow passage of the sun throught the sky lulls us into a sense of false security. In reality, Góngora implies, we should see our time passing as rapidly as a comet seems to pass through the sky. At the same time each daily cycle brings us ominously nearer to our death, and so the friendly sun takes on the ominous qualities of the comet which traditionally is seen as threatening disaster.

Some of Góngora's sonnets do move in a logical fashion towards a crowning final conceit. Such is the case with 'O claro honor del líquido elemento' (Millé 220) with

---

111   'Carrozas de ocho bestias, y aun son pocas/ con las que tiran y que son tiradas' (Millé 252).

its carefully structured argument whose explanation comes in the final tercet, or 'La dulce boca que a gustar convida', with its carefully controlled conceit in which the attractive moisture on the lips is converted into poison in the final line. The burlesque poem attacking the critics of the *Polifemo* (Millé 339) again follows a smooth sequence from start to finish based on the idea of the single eye of the giant. On the other hand there are also sonnets in which there seems to be no wit, such as that which because of its subject matter inevitably brings the *Soledades* to mind, 'Descaminado, enfermo, peregrino' (Millé 258).

In general terms, what one finds is that throughout the range of poetic forms practised by Góngora there are a fair number which show no wit, others in which wit is used to add a little extra spice to a poem, and others in which wit is integral to the whole conception of the poem. The first group of poems not surprisingly includes a fair number of Góngora's *romances* on the theme of love, some set in a pastoral context (Millé 3, 5, 14, 29, 30, 37, 45, 46, 50, 58, 83) others with a moorish flavour (Millé 15, 17, 23, 28, 39, 49). But as a form, the *romance* could be structured in four-line blocks each capable of bearing a conceit.[112] We can see this in the poem 'Del palacio de la primavera' (Millé 61) in which Góngora develops an ingenious series of parallels between life in the imaginary court of flowers in which the rose is queen, and life at the court of a human monarch. And as for the *romance* of *Angélica y Medoro* (Millé 48) here Góngora develops a very special bitter-sweet lyricism through a sequence of conceits in which counterbalanced symmetries abound.

In the realm of panegyric poetry Góngora typically leavens his praise with wit, whether it be in the Ode on the capture of Larache (Millé 383), or his light hearted *romance* celebrating Saint Teresa of Avila's achievements (Millé 69), or his sonnet in honour of the Sacro Monte in Granada (Millé 263), or that dedicated to Morales (Millé 256). In those poems where wit is uncharacteristically lacking the result can be heavy-handed as in his early poem in 'esdrújulos', 'Suene la trompa bélica', or just plain dull, as in the patriotic poems addressed to his native Córdoba and to Granada (Millé 383 and 244).

If we consider those poems to which the wit is central, no doubt some of them might be considered examples of Gracián's *agudeza compleja*. An obvious case in point would be the *romance* on the court of Queen Rose, mentioned above, in which, as in allegory, each individual conceit fits into a basic over all strategy. Again, the *canción* 'Qué de invidiosos montes' (Millé 388) could be said to have as a basic controlling idea the freedom of the poet's imagination. But in some Góngora's more substantial poems the place of individual conceits in the over all scheme may be less clear. Some critics have sought to make a distinction between those conceits which are structural, or 'organic', because they illuminate some general thematic idea in a

---

112   See Antonio Carreño's introduction to his excellent edition of Góngora's *Romances* (Madrid, Cátedra, 1985), pp. 30-32

poem, and those which are not. A.A. Parker in the introduction to his edition of the *Polifemo* argues that the wit in that poem is largely organic in this sense and that individual images function together in clusters and contribute in a significant symbolic way to broad themes, such as that of life and death.[113] But it is highly unlikely that all the conceits in this poem can be made to fit into such patterns, and what needs to be challenged is any assumption that those which do not are in any sense inferior.

It was Arthur Terry who established the distinction between the organic conceit, 'which has an organic function in the context, illuminating a particular theme or idea which is important either for the poem as a whole or for a substantial part of it', and what he not very felicitously called the 'ornamental' conceit, 'a self-contained piece of wit, indulged in for its own sake, which does not have any further purpose in its context'.[114] He saw a parallel between this distinction and that made by James Smith between the 'metaphysical conceit', whose elements, according to Smith, 'enter into a solid union, and at the same time maintain their separate and warring entity', and the 'merely extravagant' conceit whose elemnts 'come together only for a moment ... and then immediately fly apart'.[115] Terry's scheme, however, has the advantage of being in principle less subjective than Smith's, since the metaphorical 'flying apart' is something which may happen in one reader's mind but not another's. What is of particular interest from our point of view are two examples from Góngora with which Terry illustrates his distinction. He cites as an organic conceit some lines from *Angélica y Medoro* (Millé 48), 'tórtolas enamoradas/ son sus roncos atambores', where erotic incitement is metaphorically portrayed as a call to arms, so that the image relates to the love/war theme which is important in this poem. As an example of an ornamental conceit he offers the following lines from the *Polifemo*

> De su frente la perla es Eritrea
> émula vana; el ciego Dios se enoja,
> y condenado su esplendor, la deja
> pender en oro al nácar de su oreja. (109-112)

The second of these passages is the more complex of the two and offers a remarkable sequence of interconnected ideas which terminates in a perfect correspondence. Firstly Góngora heightens the description of Galatea's pearly complexion by hyperbolically reversing the expected comparison. Instead of thinking in terms of a brow resembling a pearl, Góngora allows the brow to set the standard and sees the pearl as failing to meet it. This leads naturally into the poetic fiction that by being worn as a dangling earring the pearl is being punished for its presumptiousness in even imagining that it can match Galatea. The punishment is seen as administered by Cupid, the blind God who ironically here is concerned with visual standards, because

113 *Polyphemus and Galatea* (Edinburgh, Edinburgh University Press, 1977), p. 57 ff.
114 Arthur Terry, 'Quevedo and the metaphysical conceit', *Bulletin of Hispanic Studies,* 35 (1958), pp. 211-222, (p. 213)
115 James Smith, 'On Metaphysical poetry', *Scrutiny,* 3 (1933), pp. 222-39

as the supreme example of loveliness, adored by all, Galatea must be matchless. Finally the sequence of ideas is capped by the brilliant correspondence between Galatea's ear and mother-of-pearl. Here, as Colin Smith has pointed out, the metaphor *nácar* is based upon an analogy of shape. It is as if the pearl, now attached to a shell-like ear, has been restored to its original home.[116] Even the very conventional metaphor of gold to describe Galatea's hair is revitalized by the appropriateness of literal gold for a piece of jewelry. In terms of the virtuosity with which it smoothly connects a variety of elements this is wit of a very high standard. If it is extravagant, it is certainly not 'merely' extravagant, and 'ornamental' seems an inappropriate term to describe it. I find myself admiring it more than some examples of so-called organic wit.

The issue here is how Góngora's conceits work together. Sometimes, as in the above example, the wit follows a complex sequence within a particular passage. We have seen other examples of this in *Las firmezas de Isabela*, or in Góngora's burlesque poem about a doctor's mule (Millé 54). Akin to these are examples where Góngora gives us a series of images in which the ability to accumulate examples formed on a similar basis is what impresses. Take Góngora's punning using culinary language to refer to the deaths of Hero and Leander. These are examples of patterns concentrated in a particular passage rather than the more diffuse larger scale symmetries.

If we look at the *Soledades*, a major showcase for Góngora's wit, it is possible to discern a common thread linking some of his images, such as the technique of making paradoxical interchanges between the four elements. But it would be wrong to assume that a uniform philosophical stance underlies such images, or that Góngora's wit in the *Soledades* is predominantly systematic. And in any event, the repetition of the same technique although it may enhance the unity of a poem does not by the same token automatically enhance the wit. The pattern produced by considering together the individual conceits may not amount to what Gracián would have considered a *correspondencia*. We are more likely to feel that an extra sharpness has been added when having established a pattern the poet diverges from it, ironically varying his theme. Such is the case, for example, when, for once Góngora uses the word 'cristal' for once to refer to glass rather than water (II, 578).

What is impressive about the wit in the *Soledades* is the brilliance of its individual perceptions, its variety, and it subtlety. The contribution made by the accumulation of individual conceits to the poem as a whole is to create a kind of emotional unity by means of the sense of amazement they generate. In a sense this makes them 'organic' in that this poem sets out to present the wide-eyed response of agreeable surprise felt by the young aristocrat encountering for the first time as the result of a shipwreck the way of life of a peasant community and their environment.

---

116   C. Colin Smith, 'An approach to Góngora's Polifemo', *Bulletin of Hispanic Studies,*
       42 (1965), pp. 230-38 (p. 223)

The presence of so many conceits manoeuvres the reader into sharing this sense of wonderment.

Each reader will have a personal list of which conceits linger most powerfully in the mind, whether it be the invitation to the Duke of Bejar to lean his ash-handled spear against an ash, or the description of a sailing boat as a sunflower of the wind ('vaga Clicie del viento' (I, 372), or of fleets of them as 'selvas inconstantes' (I, 404), the description of the view from a hilltop in terms of a map (I, 194) , or the tree with musical leaves (I, 590), or the gravity-defying athletes (I, 1029), etc., etc. The inventive drive shown by Góngora in the wit of the *Soledades* is manifested in other ways in his career as a poet. He had a unique role in his promotion of certain poetic forms, such as the hexasyllabic *romancillo*, or the *letrilla*, and was capable of giving familiar forms a novel twist, as in creating an epistolary sonnet (Millé 334), or a *romance* with rhymes instead of assonance (Millé 49). He was novel in the genres which he practised, making a unique contribution in the area of the burlesque. In terms of its genre, the *Soledades* is *sui generis*, and the same can be said of his disconcerting burlesque *romance* on Pyramus and Thisbe (Millé 74). As for *Las firmezas de Isabela,* there is no other play like it, with its bourgeois characters, and its untypical mode of exposition.[117] As Robert Jammes has noted, Góngora was always experimenting and was never content to rest on his laurels.[118]

The subtlety of Góngora's wit in the *Soledades* owes much in technical terms to his exploitation of complex trope. The advantage conferred by the use of figurative language is that it can draw our attention to a witty correspondence in passing, as it were, implying it rather than stating it outright. In this respect the use of trope is akin to the use of allusion, which is also typical of Góngora. And where things are put across by indirect means there is often room to disconcert and tease the reader. The subtle borderline between figurative and literal language is one which Góngora was particularly adept at exploiting in a way which can cause the reader to vacillate.

Again one can say that subtlety is a general hallmark of Góngora's poetry which extends beyond his use of wit. In this respect one could contrast the typical vehemence of Quevedo, which in his satrical work was capable of tilting over into sheer crudeness, and Góngora's greater detachment.

For example, in the realm of love poetry by contrast with the personal involvement of Quevedo in, say the love sonnets addressed to Lisi, Góngora often approaches love as an outsider, celebrating the loves of others, be it Acis and

---

117   See Robert Jammes' introduction to his edition of *Las firmezas de Isabela,* (Madrid, Castalia, 1965)

118   'Dès qu'il a découvert une veine, crée un modèle, lancé un style, il les abandonne por porter ailleurs ses efforts. Artiste perpétuellement insatisfait de lui-même et des autres, il n'exploite jamais ses propres découvertes...Pour rester fidèle a lui même don Luis dut résister aux pressions des amis, des libraires, et des grands personnages du royaume'. Robert Jammes, *Etudes sur l'oeuvre poétique de Don Luis de Góngora y Argote* (Bordeaux, Féret, 1967), p. 636

Galathea or Angélica and Medoro. At times there are hints of voyeurism, most obviously in 'Qué de invidiosos montes' (Millé 388), but also in his repeated use of the word 'brújula', meaning a peephole, in the context of glimpses offered of the female body, whether it be merely an foot or ankle displayed during the dance,[119] or more the more intimate charms of Góngora's lover[120], or   Galatea whose reactions are cunningly observed by Acis through half-closed eyes.[121]   One might add the curious detail of the shipwrecked young man admiring the beauty of the mountain girls from a vantage point in the hollow of a tree.[122]   Where Góngora does portray himself as a lover, it is often from a comic, detached perspective.

In the realm of personal invective, whilst Quevedo with vicious crudeness, on the assumption that his readers will share his anti-semitic prejudices, states that the size of Góngora's nose is effectively all we need to know about him[123], Góngora mocks Quevedo's pretensions to Greek scholarship in a sonnet whose humour although schatological at the end is expressed through the subtler medium of puns and *double entendres* (Millé LXII). The same kind of humour is revealed in the magnificent sonnet defending the *Polifemo* (Millé 339) in which the poem shrugs off its critics with the contemptuousness of a giant dismissing pygmies.

Góngora has a quiet self-confidence which not only allows him to stick to his guns in the face of sniping criticism, but to stand back and mock himself as a lover, as a smug provincial gentleman, even as a poet, parodying his own style on occasion. He has the inscrutability of genius.

---

119   See 'En los pinares de Xúcar' (Millé 52)
120   See 'Dejad los libros ahora' (Millé 32)
121   Lines 289-293
122   'De una encina embebido/ en lo cóncavo el joven matenía/ la vista de hermosura' (I, 267-9)
123   'Yo te untaré tus obras con tocino', *Obras completas,* ed. Blecua, p. 1171

Index of Names

Index of Citations

Index of Subjects

Further Reading from Aris & Phillips

Francisco de Quevedo (1580-1645)
DREAMS AND DISCOURSES *(Sueños y discursos)* by R. K. Britton (Barnsley).
'Quevedo's *Sueños* his moral and civic sermons, often make painful reading
because, for all their brilliant language and style, ingenious presentation, and
psychological insights, the festering resentment shows through. ...This agreeable
new translation is very welcome and the editor is to be congratulated for undertaking
so daunting a task. His useful introduction puts Quevedo and his writings into
context and the helpful notes clarify some of the intricate problems in this difficult
work.' *Modern Language Review cloth 0 85668 3523; paper 0 85668 353 1 (1989)*

CICERO – Philosophical works
ON FATE *and* BOETHIUS CONSOLATION OF PHILOSOPHY Book V, edited
by R.W. Sharples *(London) cloth 0 85668 475 9, limp 0 85668 476 7 (1992)*
ON STOIC GOOD AND EVIL: *De Finibus* 3 and *Paradoxa Stoicorum* edited by
M.R. Wright *(Reading)* 'a very good and clear brief account of Hellenistic
philosophy' *G. & R. cloth 0 85668 467 8, limp 0 85668 468 6 (1991)*
LAELIUS ON FRIENDSHIP and THE DREAM OF SCIPIO: *Laelius De Amicitia*
and *Somnium Scipionis*, edited by J.G.F. Powell *(Newcastle)* 'could be used
profitably by anyone interested in Roman Philosophy' *Class.World cloth 0 85668
440 6, limp 0 85668 441 4 (1991)*

HORACE
SATIRES I, edited by P.Michael Brown *(Glasgow) cloth 0 85668 529 1, limp 0
85668 530 5 (1993)*
SATIRES II, edited by Frances Muecke *(Sydney) cloth 0 85668 531 3, limp 0 85668
532 1 (1993)*
Horace's verse-satires are the earliest fully extant example of the genre in European
literature; he not only handles moral topics with a persuasive air of sweet reason but
also reveals much of his own engaging personality and way of life.

SENECA
FOUR DIALOGUES: *Consolatio ad Helviam, De Tranquillitate Animi, De Vita
Beata, De Constantia Sapientis* edited by C.D.N. Costa *(Birmingham)*
Seneca's Dialogues were an important medium for the spreading of Greek
philosophical theories to the Roman world and to subsequent ages. This selection is
of complete, not excerpted, dialogues and gives a fair idea of the range of Seneca's
philosophical interests and of his didactic techniques.
cloth 0 85668 560 7, limp 0 85668 561 5 (1994)

Catalogues of our books in Oriental, Classical and Hispanic literature
are available from: ARIS & PHILLIPS Ltd, Teddington House,
Warminster, Wiltshire BA12 8PQ England

RE-READING HISPANIC LITERATURE
A series of monographs dedicated to work by contemporary British scholars.

Ruth Christie, Judith Drinkwater, John Macklin *(Leeds)*
THE SCRIPTED SELF: Textual Identities to Contemporary Spanish Narrative
The period since 1975 in Spain, following years of dictatorship, has seen a remarkable surge of creative cultural activity. Particularly significant has been the proliferation of novels by both new and established writers, often termed *nueva narrative española,* in which, for example, *novela negra, novela erótica, novela documental* and *novela 'light'* co-exist. From within this diversity, the recurrent themes of self and identity emerge as a constant preoccupation and constitute the central concern of this new study. Christie, Drinkwater and Macklin read their chosen texts in terms of the possibilities and limits of writing the self. New narrative writing in Spain addresses the absence at the heart of concepts of identity and self, exploring and dissecting societal norms, cultural codes and inherited discourses in a period of rapid economic and political change. *ISBN O 85668 664 6 limp (1995)*

Helen Wing and John Jones *(Hull)*
BELIEF AND UNBELIEF IN HISPANIC LITERATURE, *papers from a Conference at the University of Hull, 12 and 13 December 1994.*
The number, nature and range of the contributions bears witness to the multi-faceted importance of religion in Hispanic literature and culture and to the recognition of this in current research in Hispanic Studies. The papers here presented cover areas extending from the Spanish Golden Age to contemporary Catalan and Spanish-American writing. They show the continuing preoccupation with religion; in some works through the incorporation of religious themes and imagery which affect their form and content; in others through their embodiment and expression of religious convictions and views which reinforce the dominant culture; yet in others, through the ways in which that culture is challenged and subverted by the transgression of established religious ideas and principles. This volume will encourage further exploration and exchange of ideas on this vast and immensely rich field. *ISBN 0 85668 656 5 limp (1995)*

Barry Jordan
BRITISH HISPANISM and the Challenge of Literary Theory.
Dr Jordan considers some basic questions of literary and cultural theory and critical practice, as applied to the teaching of literary studies in modern languages. *ISBN 0 85668 515 1 limp (1990)*